f*ck no!

Also by Sarah Knight

**THE LIFE-CHANGING MAGIC OF
NOT GIVING A F*CK**

GET YOUR SH*T TOGETHER

YOU DO YOU

CALM THE F*CK DOWN

GET YOUR SH*T TOGETHER JOURNAL

CALM THE F*CK DOWN JOURNAL

f*ck no!

how to stop saying yes
when you can't, you shouldn't,
or you just don't want to

sarah knight

VORACIOUS

Little, Brown and Company

New York   Boston   London

Voracious / Little, Brown and Company
Hachette Book Group
1290 Avenue of the Americas, New York, NY 10104
littlebrown.com

First Edition: December 2019

Voracious is an imprint of Little, Brown and Company, a division of Hachette Book Group, Inc. The Voracious name and logo are trademarks of Hachette Book Group, Inc.

The publisher is not responsible for websites (or their content) that are not owned by the publisher.

The Hachette Speakers Bureau provides a wide range of authors for speaking events. To find out more, go to hachettespeakersbureau.com or call (866) 376-6591.

Illustrations and hand lettering by Lauren Harms

ISBN 978-0-316-52914-3
LCCN 2019952529

10 9 8 7 6 5 4 3 2 1

LSC-C

Printed in the United States of America

Contents

||

BECOMING A NO-IT-ALL: How to say no to pretty much anything   **95**

INVITATIONS: Fancy fêtes, informal gatherings, opening nights, shamanic rituals, and joining the club   **97**

f*ck no!

What the world needs now is no, sweet no

Why is it so fucking hard to say *no*?

How did the act of uttering one little word become more difficult than all the stuff we wind up doing because we couldn't, wouldn't, or felt we shouldn't... just politely decline?

What makes us pack our calendars full and drain our bank accounts empty instead of expressing a simple "Can't make it" or "Not today" or "I'm sorry, young lady, but I don't like Girl Scout cookies. They taste like unhappy sand."

I've thought a lot about these questions since I wrote my first book, *The Life-Changing Magic of Not Giving a Fuck: How to Stop Spending Time You Don't Have with People You Don't Like Doing Things You Don't Want to Do.* For years, I've shouted my core belief all over bookstores and on podcasts and TV and radio interviews throughout the world: that **it's your right to live on your own terms.** You can opt out of events, tasks, expenditures, obligations, or even relationships that don't make you happy, and you needn't feel guilty for doing so. In other words — **it's okay to say no whenever you goddamn please, to whomever you goddamn must, and you don't have to be so goddamn sorry about it.***

By far the most common inquiry I get from readers, listeners, and strangers in my Instagram DMs is this:

> **I understand you're telling me it's *okay* to
> say no — but how do I do it?
> Like, literally, *HOW???***

You might be wondering the same thing.

In fact, I'm guessing you picked up *Fuck No!* because you're looking for ways to bridge that powerful divide between **the pull of wanting to say no** and **the pressure of feeling like you have to say yes.**

Maybe you're feeling the burn of taking on too many assignments at work or too many projects for school or too much emotional labor at home.

Maybe, like my friend Lauren, you've racked up hundreds of dollars in overseas roaming fees because you can't say no to the Democratic National Committee when they robocall you repeatedly during your vacation.

Maybe you even tried saying no once or twice when it really mat-

---

* I believe this so hard that I invented an entire strategy — the NotSorry Method — for accomplishing it. More on that later.

tered to you, and it didn't go very well. There were dirty looks or guilt trips or tears, and so you caved, **resigning yourself to a life of yes because it's "easier" in the moment.**

Oh, honey. *No.*

But listen, I get it. While I did write an entire book that the aptly named magazine *Real Simple* said "will lighten your spirit and clear your calendar, freeing up time and energy for yourself (and your Netflix account)," I acknowledge that *The Life-Changing Magic of Not Giving a Fuck* was primarily focused on **getting to no *in your own mind.***

And since you need to be able to say no to yourself before you can say it to anyone else, *Fuck No!* will double down on some of these best practices. Among the newer, no-ier concepts, I'll offer petite primers on **fuck bucks and the budgeting thereof, mental decluttering, personal policies,** and everyone's favorite guilt-free pleasure: my **Not-Sorry Method.**

Then I'm going to take it all one giant leap further, into **real, live, practical application** — that is, **saying no *to other people's faces*** (and voicemail and inboxes and pre-printed RSVP cards, and more).

Oh, YES.

Mark my naughty words, you hold in your hands a veritable **encyclopedia of examples** containing a **cornucopia of comebacks** and a **plethora of polite replies.** There are at least four-hundred-and-fifteen distinct ways to say *no, nein,* and *non merci.** It has charts! And graphics! And an exercise of fill in the blank words, which is akin to Mad Libs™

---

* Many more, in fact, but I got tired of counting.

and which is not called Mad Libs™ because the name Mad Libs™ belongs to someone else.

From the daily concerns of adding events to your calendar and to-dos to your list; to the infrequent but no less burdensome prospects of being expected to plan your twenty-fifth high school reunion just because you were the class president <checks calendar> twenty-five years ago, or executing a too-big project on a too-short deadline; to the rare request to be your BFF's sperm donor — **if you WANT to say no but can't find the words to actually, literally, definitively SAY SO, it will be my pleasure to put them in your mouth.**

Have you been invited to a dog's birthday party, perchance?

Or been asked to take on additional work for no additional pay?

Does your landlord want to raise your rent without fixing the water heater?

Are you feeling pressured by an overzealous stylist into changing your lewk?

Do your parents wish you would at least *consider* having that tattoo removed before your sister's wedding?

Never fear, I will show you **how to say a firm-yet-pleasant no** to all of these enervating entreaties, and more.

I say no all the time — to my friends and family, to prospective clients, and to producers who want me to get up before my customary 10:30 a.m. to appear on their morning radio shows three time zones back. Sometimes I propose an alternative; sometimes I take a hard pass. In any case, practice makes perfect, and this book represents the full length and breadth of my *No* files — one of which is bound to apply to that bar mitzvah you've been hoping to avoid for the last twelve years.

Yes, these days saying no is kinda my specialty. But my life wasn't always *No thanks!* and *Fuck that!*

No, no it wasn't.

I no whereof I speak

Before I became an internationally renowned setter-of-boundaries, **I was the poster child for saying yes when I really wanted to say no** — only to be left wondering why in God's name I'd thought "Sure, I can host your baby shower!" was easier and better than simply having found a nice way to decline. (If you're at all familiar with my work, this example *in particular* should be an indication that I was not operating in my current no-fucks-given state of mind.)

Well into my thirties, I was **a next-level people-pleaser.** Day in and day out, you'd hear me say "Yep, no problem" and "Okay, I can do that!"

Even when it *was* a problem and I *couldn't* do it.

Or *shouldn't* do it.

Or just didn't *want* to do it.

Sometimes I felt powerless in the face of peer pressure. **Sometimes**

I put too much pressure on myself. And all too often I didn't listen to the little voice in my head warning me that saying yes was a bad idea; I said it anyway and hoped it wouldn't be *that* bad.

Reader, it was almost always *that* bad.

A brief list of things I regret having agreed to during those first three-plus misspent decades includes but is not limited to:

- Doing other people's homework
- Lying to cover for a friend
- Having sex with an awful person
- Hiking
- Eating sushi
- Taking jobs for less money than I was worth
- Starting a doomed sci-fi imprint at the last publishing house I worked for
- Letting someone else book plane tickets on my behalf that resulted in me traveling from Montana to New York via SEATTLE

(Truly, you haven't lived until you've spent two hours flying west wedged next to a panicking lady of indeterminate illness who forgot to pack her medication, only to land at Sea-Tac for a five-hour layover before backtracking across the country on a redeye to Newark.)

Eventually, all those regrettable yeses — and thousands more — accumulated to induce my own personal breaking point. I wouldn't say

I *snapped,* exactly, but I did quit my fifteen-year career as a book editor in New York City to go freelance and move to a minuscule Caribbean town where there are approximately 8.6 million fewer people who could possibly ask me to do shit with or for them in any given day.*

In the process of making those major life changes, I found myself saying some **Big, Existential No's**: to long-held expectations for my career and future; to the pace and pressure of the city, but also to the comfort and convenience of the first world; to being cold; and to ever again donning Spanx for any reason.

Ironically, it was only after I'd done all that heavy lifting that I realized **how many (hint: MANY) smaller but no less significant no's were on the table:**

Add an unnecessary item to my to-do list? *No.*

Pencil an unwanted event into my calendar? *No thank you.*

Spend an ungodly amount of money to do something unenjoyable? *Fuck no!*

To be fair, maybe once you've bailed on a job, a home, and a country all within six months, you get a little trigger happy, but I have to say this approach has been working out well for me. Not only is my life now largely free of shit I can't or shouldn't or don't want to do,

---

* If you didn't already know that part of my backstory, well, now you have context when I start talking about "my old corporate life" and the bountiful palm trees, lizards, and feral cats currently inhabiting my yard.

I've had more opportunities to say a sincere, enthusiastic *Yes!* to things that I find interesting, engaging, and important — and to do them happily and well.

For example, by opting out of the strict schedule of corporate life, I've been able to nurture new friendships in my new hometown over no-pressure lunches in the middle of my self-designed workday. By devoting less of my brain power to petty office grievances, I've been able to use more of it to learn Spanish. And by spending less money on the privilege of existing in New York City, I've been able to put more toward causes that I admire. All fab outcomes.

Most significantly, since the Great Personal and Professional Meltdown of 2015 I've published five No Fucks Given Guides, two journals, and a page-a-day calendar full of **profanity-laden advice pertaining to mental health and happiness.** (The *Observer* dubbed me "the anti-guru," a moniker I find fitting and delightful.) This has been both a dream come true AND a test of my ability to say no when I need to; as it turns out, because all of my publisher-sanctioned tomfoolery happens on a fairly punishing timeline, I'm not much less busy than when I was people-pleasing my way up the corporate ladder in New York.

Aha! you might be thinking. *You said no and wound up right back where you started. There's no hope for the rest of us!*

Not so fast there, Carl Lewis.

Yes, I'm still busy with **stuff I *want* and *need* to do.** The difference is that now **I'm comfortable saying no to all the other stuff** that would make my life *even busier* and/or *less enjoyable*.

I mean, I could continue to let feelings of guilt and obligation push me into saying yes to every invitation I receive or favor that's asked of me when I'm on deadline—and I might still get my books turned in on schedule because I'm a type A perfectionist who is constitutionally incapable of not doing so—but I'd also be making myself miserable in the meantime.

No thanks!

And **saying no isn't only about sacrificing fun or blowing off other people's needs** because you can't say yes to it/them without royally fucking up your own life.

That's just the beginning.

Saying no is about **setting and protecting all kinds of boundaries—even when you technically *can* say yes, but you *shouldn't*** (see above: "I might still meet my deadline, but I'd also be making myself miserable in the meantime") or frankly, **you could, but you *just don't want to.***

That's right frogs and toads: I say no to invites and activities and vacations and objectively lovely and enticing offers not because I have something *better* or *more important* to do, but because I. DO. NOT. WANT. TO. DO. *THAT.* THING.

Do I still feel a twinge of guilt when friends invite me out to dinner and instead of saying yes because it's a nice of them to ask and it'll probably be fun and I don't really have anything else to do, I say no because to be honest I'd rather eat an entire container of hummus and go to bed at 9 p.m. accompanied by half an Ambien and a thick layer of under-eye moisturizer?

Sure I do. Anti-gurus are only human.

But as with any exercise that requires willpower — like sticking to a diet or fitness regimen, quitting smoking, or refraining from reaching across the table to murder a loud chewer — I try to **focus on the long-term benefits** even when it feels difficult, wrong, or unnatural in the short term. Plus, **I no longer view "no" as a negative** (disappointing people, rejecting friends, missing out on fun); **I see it as a positive** (relaxing, having some alone time, getting sleep or getting work done, whatever it may be).

It's a revelation, I tell you.

Through trial and error, and buoyed by the fruits of my early success, I've trained myself to get past the initial discomfort and say no whenever I need to for my own well-being — whether it's because **I CAN'T** do something, or **I SHOULDN'T**, or **I JUST DON'T WANT TO.** Otherwise it's my own fault that I'm munching on an Outback Steakhouse Bloomin' Onion for the third time in a week just because my coworkers asked me to join them for happy hour and I couldn't figure out how to say "Not tonight, thanks!"

(That was a hypothetical example, as I currently live in a tiny fishing village in the Dominican Republic where there are no chain restaurants and I have no coworkers. But you get my drift.)

Anyway, all of this is to say that Shonda Rhimes can have her *Year of Yes.* I'm super happy with my life of no.

And you could be too.

Turning the status quo into status: no

Together, we're going to **reframe the conversation, defang the word, and destigmatize the act of saying *nyet*.***

You'll stop thinking about "no" as too hard, wicked rude, and just plain unacceptable, and start thinking about it as pretty easy, perfectly polite, and eminently justifiable, actually.

Like a bowl of carbs before a big night out, part I of this book lays a base — of **theory, strategy, and technique** for all of the hands-on work to come. It includes:

- Why do I say yes all the goddamn time? (a quiz)
- The Why Yes/When No Method
- Different nopes for different folks
- The Power No
- Setting boundaries
- Guilt: a few observations
- Do I really *have* to? (a flowchart)
- How to say what you really mean without being really mean
- A practice round featuring neighbors, vendors, and people you never liked in high school and still don't

---

* That's Russian for "no." As in "No, I won't accept foreign interference in this election." WAS THAT SO DIFFICULT.

- The joy of no

- And plenty of No-Tips for all occasions!

In part II, we'll put all of the above to good use. Chapter by chapter, I'll provide **hundreds of concrete examples of things you might want or need to say no to,** how to do it, and what you stand to gain.

HUNDREDS, I TELL YOU.

And *Fuck No!* isn't just a compendium of sassy comebacks and salty f-bombs. (Though it is that too.) I want you to walk away from this book with a deeper appreciation for **how much better your life can be when you say no with confidence** — and without guilt, stigma, fear, and regret.

I want to **transform the way we approach invitations** — viewing them as welcoming offers, not intimidating obligations. I want us to **feel good about doing favors when we can, and stop feeling bad about it when we can't.** I want to help you **eliminate the things you shouldn't be doing, so you can enjoy and succeed at those you should.** I want families to **listen to and communicate better with one another** — especially the ones and others who just don't want to show up every time, for every occasion.

Along the way, we'll discuss:

No **is an option.** And it isn't just for RSVP cards. It's for colleagues who ask you to cover for them for the third time this week. It's for second cousins seeking interest-free loans. It's for bosses who want you to work too much and clients who want to pay too little. It's for kids and dates and roommates and phone solicitors and third tequila shots.

No **is a bargaining chip.** Saying it can get you fewer commitments and less hassle — but it could also get you more, like a raise or a promotion. It all depends on how you wield it. I'll give you lots of variations to bring to the table.

No **is a tool for change.** Consent is one of the most pressing issues of our time, and everyone can use an extra lesson in how to give, withhold, and identify it. I'll address the importance of setting and enforcing boundaries (intimate and otherwise) and celebrate your right and privilege to do so.

Ultimately, I want to help you **re-envision what it means to** *give* *no* **as your answer,** and then go out there and do it so **other people have to re-think what it means to** *take* **no for an answer.**

We're all in this together, folks. We need to get comfortable saying no for our own health and the health of our relationships with family, friends, lovers, bosses, colleagues, clients, landlords, roommates, students, teachers, teammates, coaches, and everyone else who needs to hear it.

No **is an acceptable answer.** It's time to start using it.

1

IT'S A YES-OR-NO QUESTION:

Deciding which answer is best for you

To kick things off, we'll look **at all of the reasons people say yes when they want to say no** — and more specifically, all of *your* reasons.

Are you a **classic people-pleaser?** Do you, to your detriment, worry more about others than about yourself? Are you **afraid of missing out** — on fun, or opportunities, or just "likes" on Instagram? Is it your intention to **overachieve?** Or at the end of the day, are you just **a big fucking pushover?** (Forgot to mention: if you thought you were going to get through this book without having to fess up to your hang-ups, then you don't know me very well.)

Next, we'll **meet your nemeses, the Yes-Men,** and I'll show you **four simple, reliable paths into the No Zone** — plus some bonus techniques with which to enact **expert-level naysaying.** And because we all live in the real world with problems and challenges that must be confronted even when we don't feel like it, I'll also offer guidelines for figuring out **when you really *have* to say yes.**

Do you smell a flowchart? BECAUSE I SURE DO.

We'll get all up in your **boundaries;** we'll talk about **guilt;** we'll talk about **shifting your mind-set;** and I'll lay down a strategy borne from my earlier studies in Not Giving a Fuck that also serves as **the gold standard for How to Say No.** Then I'll show you how you can massage it to suit your unique circumstances, because silver and bronze standards never hurt anybody.

After that, **a practice round to get your juices no'ing,** and I'll close out part I by giving you a glimpse at the greater good — **the**

ways in which you saying no can improve lives other than your own. (Feel free to pretend that's all you're reading it for. I won't tell.)

Meanwhile, time to open your mind and sharpen your tongue. From this page forward, yes is on *no*-tice.

No your enemy

When you say yes all the time, you get **overwhelmed, overbooked, overdrawn, and burnt-the-fuck-*out*.** But you know that already, or you wouldn't be here. So instead of focusing on the effect, let's investigate the cause.

What motivates you to take the circuitous path to Burnout Town instead of hopping the express train to No-ville?

Perhaps you identify as a **people-pleaser,** which is not in itself a terrible quality. Aren't you reliable, helpful, and my, such a team player! But if you spend your days doing shit only because you feel like you "should," or wanting people to like you even if it kills you, well, maybe it *is* a little bit terrible.

Just calling 'em like I see 'em.

But I've been there, and in the spirit of airing out our hang-ups, I'll tell you I've had a hard time saying no for other reasons too. For example, I'm **competitive;** I don't like to admit defeat and sometimes saying no can feel like a loss. Also, I've been known to equate being busy with being virtuous, and I take pride in being the kind of gal you can rely on to get shit done. (Whether that pride is worth the extraordinary effort expended to attain it is, as they say, the rub.)

So how about you?

Or for starters, the collective "you" that formed the basis for my inspiration and conclusions throughout the book.* As I was writing

---

* A book that should in no way be considered academically rigorous or

Fuck No!, **I conducted an anonymous survey** that asked people what their motivations are for saying yes when they really want to say no. (It has not escaped me that this feedback was gathered from a bunch of people who said "yes" to taking an online survey. I appreciate you suckers.)

Among the most popular responses were:

I feel like I have no choice.

I feel guilty.

I don't want to be rude.

I don't want to seem lazy.

I'm worried I'll regret it.

I'm just a pushover.

If any of these sound familiar, then I'm here to tell you— specifically, YOU—that you *do* have a choice and you *can* say no without feeling guilty, being rude, appearing lazy, getting walked all over, or burning out for fear of missing out.

But first, you need to **figure out why you say yes all the goddamn time.**

---

scientifically sound, FYI. My publisher likes it when I get that little detail out of the way up front.

The Yes-Men cometh

After communing with all of the hang-ups and insecurities and micro-masochisms revealed by my survey, I created four categories that will serve as your baseline diagnostic throughout *Fuck No!*:

The People-Pleaser

The Overachiever

The FOMO'er

The Pushover

These are the Yes-Men. Which one are you?

We're going to spend this section figuring it out, and the rest of the book learning what to do about it. But as you read through the descriptions in the following pages, **don't get fixated on your first inkling of recognition and then skip over the rest.** We all contain multitudes.

For example, I myself am a People-Pleasing Overachiever (or a recovering one, anyway). I've never identified as a Pushover, but there's a first time for everything, so I won't rule it out. And as for FOMO ("fear of missing out," in the commonly understood manner of missing out on something fun), I'm honestly content to let other people go to parties and stuff without me. I am exceedingly fond of my couch. But I do experience that *I-should-say-yes-when-I-want-to-say-no* feeling in other ways — like when it comes to missing out on a business opportunity. I worry that if I say no this time, I may be closing a potentially lucrative door forever; it's not that I want it now, so much as I don't want to *not have the option* to want it in the future.

(Weirdly though, while I can think of several occasions when I should not have said yes to an "opportunity" that turned out to be a total clusterfuck, I can't immediately call to mind a situation in which I've regretted saying no. Huh. Interesting.)

Anyway, let's meet the Yes-Men, shall we?

The People-Pleaser

You say yes when you want to say no because...

You hate to disappoint others. You feel obligated. You feel guilty. You want people to like you and/or you don't want to be rude. You're a legit nice person who is sometimes too nice for your own good. You say yes to friends and family in need, but also to enemies, strangers, and Jehovah's Witnesses just so they won't feel bad. You agree to dates you're not interested in and you do favors like they're going out of style.

> **Things People-Pleasers should be saying instead of yes**
>
> "You go ahead without me."
>
> "I don't like Thai food. Let's get something else."
>
> "I can't afford it."
>
> "I'm sorry but no, those pants don't look right on you."

Saying no instead will help you . . .

Place much-needed value on your own happiness. You'll stop being taken advantage of by people who don't have your best interests at heart. You'll gain more downtime, plus the energy to enjoy it. **Become a Me-Pleaser!**

The Overachiever

You say yes because . . .

You might as well be the one to do it because you'll do it best. You're a perfectionist. You don't want anyone to think you're being lazy. You enjoy getting credit. You're competitive with others and/or always looking to outdo yourself, so you take on extra assignments, elaborate projects, and insane deadlines like you're sitting on the world's largest supply of Adderall. Your desire to totally crush it sometimes means you get totally crushed.

Saying no instead will help you . . .

Delegate more and panic less. You'll stop being resigned to "doing it all" and get excited about "doing what you want." You'll be able to focus

---

Things Overachievers should be saying instead of yes

"I don't have time right now."

"That's above my pay grade."

"I don't need to look that over. I trust you."

"I'm on vacation."

---

better on fewer things, setting yourself up for success at what's most important to you. **Now *that's* an achievement.**

The FOMO'er

You say yes because...

Although you don't necessarily love the feeling of taking on too much, you're afraid of what might happen if you don't. You fear missing out on something fun, or on an opportunity that *might* be rewarding—financial or otherwise. You feel like there's something wrong with you for not wanting things that other people want. (Note: fear of what other people might think belongs upstairs in "People-Pleasers.") You're ruled by regret. You go to parties and on trips even when you're not that excited about them, and you ALWAYS take the meeting. You're overcommitted and ultimately, underwhelmed.

Saying no instead will help you...

Let go of expectations (*for* yourself and *of* others) that don't serve you. You'll eliminate anxiety about your choices and be more confident in them. And you'll be fully present for, committed to, and

> ### Things FOMO'ers should be saying instead of yes
>
> "I should trust my instincts."
> "I remember how this went last time."
> "There will be other chances."
> "I do me, and that's okay."

excited about the stuff you really want to say yes to. **Turn that FOMO into JONO ("joy of no")!**

The Pushover

You say yes because . . .

You dislike confrontation. You prefer the path of least resistance. You acquiesce to lowball offers and you can't refuse telemarketers, whining children, or manipulative cats who definitely already got fed today but are awfully cute. You're low on willpower. You're indecisive. You "go with the flow" right over the edge of the falls.

> **Things Pushovers should be saying instead of yes**
>
> "I'm not comfortable with that."
> "I am immune to your charms."
> "I'm worth more."
> "I object, Your Honor."

Saying no instead will help you . . .

Gain instead of lose (time, energy, money, success, respect . . . the list goes on). You'll follow through on your goals instead of getting sidetracked. You'll be admired for your fortitude and savvy. You'll stop giving inches and save many, many miles. **It's okay to push back.**

So those are the Yes-Men. Recognize anybody you know?

Now to really hammer this shit home, take the quiz below and choose the answer that best represents what you would do in the given situation. If you can't decide, pick two. This is just a fun diagnostic tool; I'm not submitting the results to the Nobel committee or anything.

Why do I say yes all the goddamn time? (a quiz)

Your boss offers you a promotion that comes with more responsibility and a better title, but no additional pay. You take it without arguing because:

a) I'd hate to seem ungrateful.

b) I really want those new business cards. I'll work on the raise next.

c) If I hold out for more money, my boss might change their mind about the whole thing.

d) If they could have given me a raise, they would have, right? I assume it's just not possible.

Your friend asks you to be their date to a super fancy, exclusive event. TONIGHT. You don't want to go, but you say yes because:

a) I don't want my friend to get stuck going alone.

b) I guess it's not that hard to add a party to my schedule. (Plus get a quick haircut on my lunch break.)

c) Someday I *am* going to want to go to one of these fancy parties, and if I say no for tonight, I may never get another invite.

d) My arm is easily twisted.

Your coworker asks you to pitch in on something on short notice, because they failed to get it done on time. You're annoyed, but you say yes because:

a) I always try to be helpful.

b) This is what I do. I get shit done when other people can't.

c) What if I need *their* help someday? What then?!

d) I don't know, I feel weird about calling them out.

Your kid's teacher is looking for a last-minute field trip chaperone. You don't really have time to do it on top of all your other responsibilities, but you say yes anyway because:

a) I hate leaving people in the lurch.

b) I can work it out; it'll just take a bunch of rearranging.

c) I'm worried I'll regret not going the minute I see some other parent Instagramming my kid at the science museum. (Even though we've already been there as a family. Twice.)

d) I don't know. The teacher asked nicely?

A valuable but demanding client asks you to complete a huge project on a ridiculously tight deadline. You know it will be painful, but you agree because:

a) I want to keep them happy.

b) "Ridiculously tight deadline" is my middle name.

c) If I push back on the timeline and they give this project to someone else, I could lose them as a client completely.

d) I've never said no to them in the past so I feel like I can't start now.

One of your friends always expects you to be there to deal with the fallout from their bad decisions, and they're currently experiencing their third meltdown in as many weeks. You're really busy and tempted to let this latest call go to voicemail, but you answer it because:

a) I feel guilty not picking up.

b) I want to be the kind of person who always has time for my friends no matter how busy I am.

c) If I don't answer and talk some sense into them, what if I could have finally put a stop to all this madness and didn't?

d) It's easier to take these calls than to explain to my friend why it would be great to get fewer of these calls.

Your coworkers invite you to socialize after work. You're exhausted, but you say yes because:

a) I don't want them to think I dislike them (even if I do).

b) Sleep is for the weak!

c) It *could* be a good networking opportunity.

d) They'll just keep asking until I cave anyway.

Your parents decide they want to do a family trip to the Grand Canyon. You had intended to use your vacation days (and budget) on something else this year, but you say yes because:

a) I don't want to hurt their feelings.
b) Maybe I can do both if I work overtime and plan carefully.
c) What if this is my last chance to do a trip like this with my parents before they get too old to travel?
d) I feel like I have no choice when it comes to family.

Why do I say yes all the goddamn time? (the results)

If you got mostly A's...you're a People-Pleaser

If you got mostly B's...you're an Overachiever

If you got mostly C's...you've got serious FOMO

If you got mostly D's...you're a Pushover

And if you got a healthy mix of most of the letters...you need this book more than the cast of *The Departed* needed a better dialect coach. No worries. Unlike Martin Sheen's Boston accent, this is totally normal.

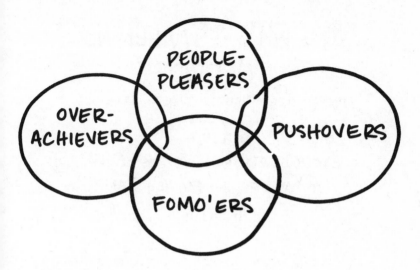

Throughout the book, I'm going to keep asking you to think about **why you may be about to say yes when you really want to say no.**

I'm doing that because you need to honestly and thoroughly confront your hang-ups at the source. Otherwise you're like those people who say "I really want to quit smoking, but it's so hard when I drink," to whom I say "Okay then, I guess smoking (i.e., saying yes) isn't your real problem. Drinking (i.e., feeling guilty/obligated/being a pushover) is. Let's work on that instead!"

Unless you don't really want to quit...?

Right. Let's carry on then.

The next time you find yourself in this predicament, pause and ask yourself WHY. I call this the **Why Yes/When No Method for Getting a Handle on Your Hang-ups.**

THE WHY YES/WHEN NO METHOD

FOR GETTING A HANDLE ON YOUR HANG-UPS

STEP 1:

ASK YOURSELF *WHY* YOU ARE ABOUT TO SAY YES *WHEN* YOU WANT TO SAY NO.

It's a really easy method, guys. One step. Give it a shot, like so:

Can I afford to give that client a discount, or am I caving just to avoid confrontation?

Should I volunteer to chair that committee, or is my ego getting more out of this than the cause?

Do I truly want to go white-water rafting, or am I just afraid of missing out on the Instagram likes? (Come on, be honest.)

Whatever your hang-ups are — guilt, obligation, pride, fear, etc. — **RECOGNIZING them is the first step to RESISTING them**; after all, how can you change your mind-set if you don't even know the current calibrations? Fortunately, when you're ready to make those changes, **there are just as many ways to say a successful no as there were reasons for relegating yourself to an ill-advised yes.** No nirvana is closer than you think.

Personally, the more I've practiced, the more comfortable I've become with a short, sweet reply vs. a long, drawn-out explanation. But I realize that's not the case for everyone — especially for a certain podcaster named Matt.

In 2018, Matt invited me on his show and we got onto the subject of saying no to people and things you don't really care about or want to do. I'd recently given a TEDx Talk on this topic, in which I'd asserted that "all you have to do is say the words *No thank you, I don't have time, I can't afford it.* You can even say *I don't want to* and trust me, the world will not end."*

Matt wasn't so sure about that.

"Could you help our listeners craft some really good 'no' statements?" he asked. "Like, beyond just a simple no — since people might be looking for something more tactful?"

I responded that in my view, **no is not tactless and over-explaining is not necessary,** but still, he persisted.

"Okay, but what if you *do* have time and you *can* afford it? What if you don't want to lie but you also want to be nice?" Matt apologized for getting,

Things that are more tactless than saying no
Sticking your tongue out
Cackling uncontrollably
Flipping the bird
Dropping your pants and giving the full moon

---

* Here's twelve minutes of your day sorted: https://tinyurl.com/yxu9exkg

as he put it, "tactical," but he remained positively thirsty for as many *specific examples* as I could toss his way.

Well, Matt, I hope you're reading. BECAUSE IT'S ABOUT TO GET TACTICAL UP IN THIS PIECE.

Different nopes for different folks

Guilt-ridden People-Pleasers, obligated Overachievers, 'fraidy cat FOMO'ers, and guess-I'm-just-a-Pushovers harbor a variety of motivations and trigger points among them, all of which can be neutralized with one of the following **four prototypes for saying no, meaning it, and being heard:**

The Hard No

Simple, direct, and nonnegotiable. This could be a straightforward *No*,* a more pleasant *No thank you,* or a slightly more explicatory *Sorry, I don't have time/can't make it/can't afford it.* In any event, your content and delivery will imply that this is the end of the conversation. Chew on that, Matt.

> **Example:** Your neighbor Ken asks if you'd be interested in helping him clean out his septic tank on Saturday. Try saying "Nope. Next question?" and I guarantee Ken will be either so flustered or so impressed by your shock-and-awe approach, he'll drop it like it's hot sewage.

---

* One word, complete sentence. No muss, no fuss.

- Pros: Gets the job done, and with minimal time and effort expended.

- Cons: A Hard No is probably the most likely to cause offense. That's not your fault, but for best results when dealing with sensitive souls, there's no harm in turning your polite meter up to eleven. (See page 62: "How to say what you really mean without being really mean.")

- Good for: Everyone, but especially People-Pleasers and Pushovers. The sooner and more clearly you can put a pin in unwanted asks and overtures, the better.

The No-for-Now

Don't confuse this with a wishy-washy "maybe" — we do not leave our friends, family, and colleagues dangling like goddamn participles. However, if you want or need to decline now, but don't necessarily wish to close off an opportunity for fun or profit *later,* this is your no, Joe.

Example (for fun): Your friends are setting up a beach timeshare this summer. It's out of your price range, but you can already feel the FOMO settling in like canned rosé at the bottom of the cooler. Instead of a Hard No, you could say "I'd love to get in on this, but I can't afford it. If you promise to ask me again next year, I'll start saving now *and* get the first case of La Croix for the house." This way, you don't blow your budget, your friends understand that you'd like another chance (for which you can prepare), and who knows — maybe someone will invite you as a weekend guest, no string bikinis attached.

Example (for profit): The family you dog-sit for has to leave town suddenly and they wonder if you're available. Unfortunately, you have a big test to cram for and this is a really bad time for you to be driving three towns over to walk Nigel the hyperactive husky three times a day. Still, you're afraid to say no and potentially lose the gig going forward. So...maybe you should just tell them that?

"Shoot, I can't do it this time, but I hope I'll still be your first call in the future — I love that crazy canine and I'd hate to lose the job over one scheduling snafu!"

- Pros: Short-term ease of use.
- Cons: Technique matters, lest you do appear wishy-washy. (See box: "Oh, I thought I responded to that already.")
- Good for: FOMO'ers and Overachievers.

No-Tip: Be explicit. Revealing your FOMO shows you're not a flake or being purposefully hard to pin down. People will be more inclined to give you another chance another time — which is what you were hoping for in the first place. And that's BOBO (best of both options)!

Oh, I thought I responded to that already.

If you'll allow me a momentary digression, one of my biggest pet peeves — resting somewhere between loud talkers on public transportation and adults riding bicycles on the sidewalks* — is when people claim they thought they already got back to me when not only did they not respond, they *know* they didn't respond, and they are now *lying about it*. That's not No-for-Now — it's just straight-up weasel. I have two friends who do this on a regular basis and let's just say one of them is not actually my friend anymore and the other one is on probation. If you don't want to do something or go somewhere or eat the worm at the bottom of the tequila bottle, just say no. It's not that hard, and I'm going to spend the rest of this book proving it if it's the last thing I thought I told you already.

The Professional No (The Pro No)

Sprinkle phrases like *As it happens* and *Upon consideration* and *I'm afraid that's unfeasible* into your emails — or, for higher degree of difficulty, learn how to say them in the moment, in person, and with a straight face.

> **Example:** A client asks if you can have their project completed two weeks ahead of schedule. If that is in fact unfeasible (or simply unappealing), you can say "Dear Eleanor, I've reviewed your file, and upon consideration, it will not

---

* If you were meant to ride your bicycle on the sidewalk it would be called a "sideBIKE," pal.

be possible to accelerate the timeline. I will certainly update you if that changes, but please expect to hear from me no later than our original deadline."

- Pros: Unimpeachably diplomatic. Ideal for workplace nopery applied broadly across bosses, colleagues, and assistants, as well as in interactions with clients, vendors, landlords, contractors, and in other business relationships.

- Cons: Perhaps a smidge too formal for use on family and friends.

- Good for: Pushovers, Overachievers, and People-Pleasers who just need a fucking break for one fucking minute.

No-Tip: It's just not possible. Especially in a work context, don't say "I'm unable" to do something. Say that something "isn't possible." This keeps your competence out of the conversation and prevents further wheedling from anyone who thinks there remains a *possibility* that you could still say yes.

The No-and-Switch

Did you know you can say no to one thing but offer an alternative thing THAT YOU PREFER? Indeed you can, Stan! The No-and-Switch is also useful when you want to avoid hurting someone's feelings, or when you actually *do* want to do something with or for them—just not in the specific manner or timeframe that they originally suggested.

Example (at work): A client asks if you can have their project completed two weeks ahead of schedule. And you could…if you get compensated accordingly. In your best Pro No vernacular, say "Dear Eleanor, I'm afraid it won't be possible to accelerate this timeline under the same terms we've agreed to. However, if you are able to increase the project budget by ten percent, I can allocate more resources to speed up completion. Please let me know within 48 hours if that is acceptable and otherwise, expect to hear from me no later than our original deadline."

Example (at play): A super-social chum often invites you to get in on urban scavenger hunts and group-discount seats for the Staten Island Yankees (or the Stankees, as I call them). You love your friend and feel bad saying no all the time, but you *don't* love all the other personality and scheduling conflicts that come with multi-person outings of this nature. You could say "Thanks for inviting me! I have to pass on [activity], but I was wondering if you and I could get together someday soon? It would be great to catch up, just the two of us!"

- Pros: You get credit for being accommodating, but in a way that works for you too.

- Cons: I wouldn't rely exclusively on the No-and-Switch. You need to say a Hard No every once in a while or people will never learn.

- Good for: Overachievers who need to dictate better terms for their success; People-Pleasers who want to help without being completely taken advantage of and have fun on mutually agreeable terms.

Schtick the landing

You'll see that I've included a healthy sprinkling of punny passes, droll declines, and witty well wishes among my sample no's. That's because I've found that lacing a no with humor can be an effective way to defuse a potentially tense situation—though I would be remiss if I did not note that turning down a job offer from an industry bigwig requires more decorum than telling your friend Leroy that he can't stay in your apartment this weekend because your building has a strict "No deadbeat stoners who let the tub overflow last time" policy. No your audience.

BONUS: the Power No

Less widely applicable than the preceding prototypes, but an equally sound solution under the appropriate circumstances, the Power No is when you issue no reply *at all*. **It's the Irish Goodbye of replies.**

I use it on strangers who slide into my DMs, wait less than a day for a response, and then send a follow-up note like "I guess you don't reply to your supporters."

Well, now I don't!

Or when someone asks for the third time about something I already said a polite no to twice. I just...stop responding. **Like ghosting, but for all the right reasons.** (For a rare, live-and-in-person use of the Power No, see page 70: "Small talk.")

Finally, the Power No is **ideal for use on people trying to worm their way back into your good graces.** For example, when someone who routinely treated my husband like shit made casual textual contact after a several-year hiatus, my advice to him was DO NOT REPLY.

Do not indulge your long-simmering animosity with a hasty *Are you fucking kidding me, you sociopathic devil-witch?* Whatever momentary satisfaction you reap will only open the door to further communication. (Sociopaths aren't known for being bothered by insults.)

Do not even send a restrained *We don't have anything to talk about.* (Sociopaths are also not known for letting go once they have a pointy Louboutin in the door.)

Do not give someone like this any satisfaction whatsoever.

My husband succeeded in holding back, and to this day it remains one of his proudest achievements. Although that garbage human better hope she never runs into me on the street, because I am not above over-processed blonde hair-pulling.

Believe me, I know it's not always easy to tamp down the impulse to chastise a pest, defend yourself from unfair accusations, or let loose a tirade that would make Lewis Black, at long last, choke on his own spit. But getting uppity provides **little short-term satisfaction with the potential for a lot of long-term aggravation.**

Whereas, if you deploy a Power No, you get to win a fight without even having it. *Neat-o.*

During the course of *Fuck No!* we'll put the Hard, Pro, and occasional Power No's through their paces, and seize many opportunities for the No-for-Now and the No-and-Switch. I'll tee up — and I believe the technical term here is "a shit ton of" — examples that range from **saying no to complete strangers** (petition-pushers, street vendors, telemarketers, etc.); **to arms-length entities** (your doctor, hairdresser, boss, colleagues, and clients); **to close personal friends and family** (including partners, children, and in-laws).

But it's no use knowing HOW to say no if you don't know WHEN to say no, is it?

Looks like it's time to set some boundaries.

The Gates of Hell No

First things first: **boundary-setting is a type of "mental decluttering,"** a concept that forms the backbone of my oeuvre. (An oeuvre that was built upon the satirizing of an extremely popular Japanese guide to physical decluttering — so, shout-out to Marie Kondo, without whom you would neither be reading this book, nor contemplating getting rid of it when you're done so as not to let it crap up your living room.)

Whether you're a returning reader or a new NFGG recruit, please see below for a wee tutorial.

Mental decluttering: a wee tutorial

Just like physical decluttering, in which you prune an overstuffed nest of possessions and arrange whatever's left to form a tidy living space, you declutter your mind in two steps: **DISCARD**, then **ORGANIZE**. From its origins in not giving a fuck to its cross-disciplinary applications in getting your shit together and calming the fuck down, we're talking about **a simple process of *deciding* and then *doing*.** In the case of this fifth and feisty No Fucks Given Guide, it's the process of **deciding to say no** — first in your own head, then **doing it** — backing up your decision with words and actions.

> **Step 1: DISCARD** (aka *decide* — what you can't, shouldn't, or don't want to say yes to). This is **SETTING YOUR BOUNDARIES.**

> **Step 2: ORGANIZE** (aka *do* — deliver your no with confidence). This is **ENFORCING YOUR BOUNDARIES.**

Make sense? Good. Now let's drill down into boundaries themselves.

What do boundaries do? **They protect things!**

What are you trying to protect? **Your time, energy, and money!**

In the parlance of the NFGGs, I refer to your time, energy, and money as your **"fuck bucks."** Like real bucks, you only have so much of each to spend before you run out or need to replenish your supply;

and therefore, in order to manage them wisely, you need a **Fuck Budget.** You probably see where I'm going with this, but just to be sure, let me spell it out:

> ***Deciding*** what's worth your time, energy, and money = ***setting*** your boundaries = ***making*** your Fuck Budget.

> ***Organizing*** your response (i.e., saying no) to what isn't worth your fuck bucks = ***enforcing*** your boundaries = ***sticking to*** your Fuck Budget.

Still with me? I hope so, because this, as Don Henley might say, is the heart of the matter.

You set boundaries to protect yourself from stuff you CAN'T or SHOULDN'T say yes to (because you don't have the fuck bucks to spare) — like posting bail for your cousin Kevin after his third DUI; **and from stuff you just DON'T WANT TO say yes to** (even if you technically do have the time/energy/money) — such as, say, going out in bad weather.

More on those examples in a minute. First, how do you wrangle your boundaries and your Fuck Budget into shape?

Consider the sheep

Think of your time, energy, and money like three prized sheep — easy prey for clever thieves and ravenous wolves, unless you, their shepherd, set some boundaries to protect them. (Yes, I'm mixing my metaphors between fuck bucks and livestock, but sheep are fun. Just go with it.)

Step 1: Establish the perimeter. First, you'll need to cordon off your precious sheep/resources with a fence. Outside the fence are all of the things being asked of you, and inside is your own personal O.K. Corral, where *yes* reigns supreme. There is a single point of entry: the Gates of Hell No.

Step 2: Enforce it. As shepherd, if you decide that something is within your Fuck Budget, you can unlock the gates and welcome the wolves and thieves (or tasks, events, and friends needing a seventh for Ultimate Frisbee) inside to feast upon your fucks. But if your budget is maxed out and your poor, overtaxed sheep are sheared down to stubble, it's up to you to protect the flock from would-be wooly bullies — including the ones in your own head who may be urging you to *Give up, Give in,* or *Give it a try; how bad could it be?* Keep those gates latched tight by saying *No way, No how, No thanks,* and *Not for me.*

Remember: setting and enforcing boundaries means **saying no TO yourself so you can say no FOR yourself.** Prevent your own Yes-Men from pilfering the coffers; then prevent other people from wandering on to your real or metaphorical property and making off with your real or metaphorical shit. Or sheep.

This perspective is especially valuable for Pushovers whose biggest problem is being indecisive. Whereas Overachievers, People-Pleasers, and FOMO'ers tend to take on too much *on purpose* (if for differing reasons), many Pushovers do it *by accident*. They wind up saying yes because they don't really know what they want, and rather than take five goddamn minutes to think about it, they just unlock the gates and wave everybody right on through.

In any case, all y'all need to work on setting some boundaries.

Ask yourself if your aforementioned drunk-ass cousin Kevin is deserving of your time, energy, and money? Do you want to grant him unfettered access to your fuzzy friends? Should you?

No?

Personal policies

A trick honed early in my not giving a fuck days that communicates your no loudly, proudly, and—best of all—in perpetuity. If your answer is *never* going to be yes to a certain request, suggestion, offer, or invitation, the flat-out easiest way to say so is "No thank you, I have a personal policy against [insert the subject of your decline]." Personal policies work because they are mysterious and also shrouded in official language. Hard to argue with and easy to defend—everything a boundary should be.

Sounds like you just set a boundary, bud. Now enforce it by telling Kev he made his own Bourbon-scented jailhouse bed and he can lie in it overnight. Or if that exact phrasing strikes you as a touch too blunt, you could whip out a **personal policy.**

Or let's say that, like me, you have little tolerance for swanning about in unfavorable weather conditions, and you get invited somewhere that you'd be subject to extreme cold, heat, or whatever. Before you say yes, ask yourself if wearing mittens or making ineffectual fans out of brunch menus is in your Fuck Budget.

No?

Boundary: set. Enforce it by telling your friend Chrissy, "They don't make deodorant strong enough to get me to a bridal shower in Palm Springs in July!"

> **Things you could tell Kevin you have a personal policy against**
>
> Lending money to relatives
> Spending more than $6,000 in one day
> Enabling unrepentant alcoholics
> Using your economic privilege to tip the scales of justice

(For what it's worth, I practice what I preach. I uprooted my entire life to move to a place where it never dips below seventy degrees and haven't attended my family's traditional Christmas festivities in Snow Central New England for three years. Don't threaten me with a winter wonderland.)

Lastly, you should know that a by-product of becoming a badass boundary-setter is that **in some cases, people will start taking the damn hint** and stop asking/expecting you to do, say, join, want, and accept things they ought to know by now are not in your Fuck Budget.*

Not a *baaa*d outcome, if I do say so myself.

Moving on, and with regard to those hang-ups I mentioned earlier, we need to address **one giant obstacle to setting and enforcing boundaries and saying no** — a nobstacle, if you will — over which I intend to help you hurdle once and for all without breaking a sweat.

Let's talk about guilt, baby

Guilt is a many splendored thing. And by "many splendored" I mean "powerful and shitty." In fact, I'd wager **guilt is the *most* powerful and *most* shitty motivator for doing things we can't, shouldn't, or don't want to do.** As such, I'd like to share some perspective from one who's been there, felt that, and managed to (*mostly*) shuck it off like a banana hammock on a nude beach.

The key is to **investigate WHY you're feeling guilty** before you allow that guilt to drive you toward saying yes when you want to say no. **Why Yes/When No**: it's not only a super-simple method, it's a multi-purpose one!

Is your guilt **warranted** (because you're doing something objectively wrong)?

---

* Sadly, some people will never get the damn hint. I'll deal with them in the next section.

Or is it **unwarranted** (because you've done nothing wrong)?

Is it purely **self-imposed** (nobody has said anything, but you still feel guilty)?

Or is it the result of **outside pressure** (other people are getting all up in your shit)?

Once you pinpoint the cause and the source, you can make more informed and appropriate decisions about **whether guilt and the assuaging thereof deserves a line item in your Fuck Budget.**

We'll begin with the most important question:

- **ARE you** *actually* **guilty (of doing something objectively wrong)?**

For example, are you contemplating stealing the last cupcake from your nephew's 3rd birthday party that you know full well your sister was saving for her breakfast tomorrow? If so, you should know it's wrong and you should feel bad about it. If you don't and you're not, then you're a real psycho.

And if you'd prefer to stop feeling guilty, THEN DON'T DO IT.

However, let's say you're contemplating not going to the party at all. You like cupcakes but you don't like getting up at 10 a.m. to watch a cut-rate clown terrify a bunch of toddlers into forgetting their potty training. Your sister may be as or more miffed as she would have been by the cupcake heist, but in this case yours is not an *objectively wrong* action. It's just you, withholding your fuck bucks from things that don't make you happy. No harm, no foul.

Furthermore, by not going, you're basically providing at least one extra cupcake for the group; two if you are then not present to steal the last one. You're awesome. And you are neither guilty *of* doing something wrong, nor should you feel guilty *about* your decision.

- **Do you FEEL guilty anyway?**

I'm not surprised. Feeling guilty even when you haven't done anything wrong is a common conundrum. But take heart, for these are precisely the mental shackles from which *Fuck No!* attempts to free you! Next question:

- **Is somebody else putting pressure on you to feel guilty?**

In most cases, I bet you're not even giving anyone else a chance to make you feel guilty about saying no, are you? You're just letting what you *think* other people think (or egad, what they *might* think) dictate your actions. I know how your mind works. But based on my years of professional experience as a giver of no fucks, I can tell you this: **Most people do not care nearly as much about how you live your life as you think they do.**

I came to this conclusion after taking the *no* plunge myself, shedding events, tasks, and people from my life and experiencing ZERO negative repercussions. It's been liberating for me and shockingly inconsequential for everyone else: a win-win!

> I have RSVP'd no to the kinds of invitations (yes, even weddings) that my sense of guilt told me were mandatory, and no one has batted so much as a disapproving eyelash in my direction.

I have summoned the wherewithal to say "I'm sorry I'm not able to be of help" to requests for favors that I don't have the time or energy to grant, and the person on the other end has responded "No worries!"

I have backed away from tasks, commitments, and interactions that I once thought were obligatory and that turned out to have been optional all along. Nobody said a peep.

- **Most of the time, the guilt is coming from inside the house.**

We'll call it 75 percent of the time. And I am telling you that if you're able to **ignore the whispers that originate in your very own brain,** you can and will be released you from the struggle of saying yes because you "feel guilty" even when you haven't done anything wrong.

Then I'm going to give you 5 percent for the things you *know* are wrong and you are *correct* to feel guilty about but that you're doing anyway, not because you're a psychopath but because shit happens and you've got to look out for Number One. I empathize.

Finally, we have the other 20 percent:

- **You've done nothing wrong, but other people still make passive-aggressive comments to express their incredulity and/or disapproval.**

They say things like "Oh, you're really not taking a shift on neighborhood watch?" or "Wow, you think it's okay to skip the christening?" Or "What kind of person doesn't like picnics?"

Such comments used to weaken my resolve, and I would let

myself be guilted into saying yes to things I couldn't, shouldn't, or didn't want to do. But now I've cultivated a perspective that's helped me rise above the fray and refuse to take the blame bait.

Remember those whispers of self-imposed guilt I told you to ignore? These people are still listening. They're projecting *their own insecurities* onto you — because they think *they're* not allowed to bow out, sit out, and opt out. **Pity them, for they no not what they do.**

Listen to their comments; then let them roll off your back. Lower your hackles. Open your arms. Release that guilt into the air like a sack of motherfucking doves. If you can ignore the voices in your head, you can ignore the voices in their heads too.

Sticking to your guns does not make you a bad person. Moreover, you can be an extra *good* person by doing your part to normalize the act of saying no. **Be the no you want to hear in the world!** The more you say it, and the happier and more guilt-free you are about it, the more people in your orbit will observe and internalize that happiness.

I've experienced this phenomenon firsthand for years now. Consciously or subconsciously — and does it really matter? — **people start to *envy* your happiness and wish to replicate it for themselves.** They, too, begin dipping their toes in the ocean of no and they, too, discover that it is thoroughly refreshing.

All of that said, this brings me to the final thing I want you to know about guilt and how you can deal with it:

● **Some people just won't quit.**

They refuse to take no for an answer. They argue your decisions ad nauseam. They huff, they puff, and they insist that you are not allowed to think about and value things differently than they do — up to and including your own time, energy, money, and sanity.

You have three options to deal with such folks:

Ignore them. Just like you're starting to ignore the voices in your own head and the offhand comments from others who don't know any better.

Acknowledge them. Respond with a simple "I've heard what you have to say, but it doesn't change my mind about going to your boyfriend's third open mic night this week. I don't think this makes me a bad person. I hope you agree, but either way, I'm done talking about it."

Engage with them. Ask why they are so intent on you saying yes to something they know you can't, shouldn't, or don't want to do? Posit that perhaps their refusal to take no for an answer says more about them than it does about you. Inform them that you refuse to feel guilty — or be *made* to feel guilty — about making decisions in service to your own happiness and well-being, such as not using your entire annual allotment of vacation days to sleep on a cot and do morning trust falls at the "adult summer camp" your mother so forcefully wishes for you to attend with all the cousins.

And you can do it all with a big ol' smile on your face, imbued as you are with the peace and satisfaction of living your life in the way that works best for you. Namaste.

So that was **guilt**. Next stop on our Magical Hang-up Tour: **obligation!**

But what if I really *can't* say no?

On your journey to saying confident, successful, objectively justifiable and guilt-free nos — to yourself or to anyone else — you'll need to separate whether you are **ACTUALLY obligated** to do something, or if you're just **FEELING obligated.**

Sound familiar?

And for the sake of my upcoming argument, let's assume this is an obligation (or "obligation") that **you can but do not *want* to fulfill.** Despite that —

Is this an "**I know I *must* do it anyway**" — like giving a presentation at work because it is your literal job to do so?

Or just an "**I feel like I *should* do it anyway**" — such as volunteering for a committee at work because you feel guilty not doing so, even though it's optional?

And if it's an "**I feel like I *should*,**" well... ***will* you?** Even if you're not technically obligated?

Oof. These mental ministrations can be taxing, especially that last one.

I hear you, my tender chickens, and I want to help — but ultimately **it's YOU who must determine whether you really, truly *have to* or *should* say yes,** or whether that instinct is borne from the guilty, obligated ramblings of your inner People-Pleasing, Overachieving, FOMO Pushover. (It probably is.)

If I try to account for each and every one of those permutations in each and every example throughout the book, it's going to get messy and digress-y real quick. But like I said, I want to help, so for now I'm going to walk you through a couple of sample scenarios and give you **a set of guidelines that you can apply to all of your future yes-or-no needs.**

Let it never be said that I am not a full-service anti-guru.

Must I? Should I? Will I?

What if your boss asks you to do something you feel like you *shouldn't have to do,* but you're worried you *do have to do it* if you want to keep your job? Or if a family member asks you to do something *you don't want to do,* but you feel like *you should do it* just to keep the peace, or because in the grand scheme of things, doing it would help them more than it would hurt you?

In the end, *will you* do it?

These questions should help get you to your answer:

- **Do you know the consequences of saying no here?**

  Has your boss said "If you don't do X, I will find someone who can!" Or do you just *assume* you have to do everything your boss asks you to do under penalty of firing, even though you've never actually tried saying no to them and seeing what happens?

Has your sister said "If you don't do X, I will never forgive you!" Or are you just *anticipating* that she'll be upset (and letting it make you feel guilty) even though she's given no indication that saying no to X would be a sororal deal-breaker?

And what have we already discussed re: preemptive, self-imposed guilt? Hmm?

- **If you *don't know* the consequences of saying no, how much of your impulse to say yes is rooted in logic and reality, and how much resides only in your irrational imagination?**

If your boss has not laid down any concrete consequences for defying them, but you have seen them yell at or threaten to fire other people, then you can logically infer that they might yell at or threaten to fire you too. You'll have to weigh your options accordingly (below).

But if you've never once seen your boss snap — and especially if you've watched Terry from the next cubicle say no to shit like this a million times with no fallout — then consider why YOU are tempted to say yes to X. (Why Yes/When No? The fun never ends with this one!)

Is it because you think doing it will be easier than saying no? (Pushover.) Or because you want to look better than Terry and/ or be seen as the Person Who Can Do It All Even When It Hurts? (Overachiever.) Maybe revisit your quiz results to suss out your motivation here.

And while we're at it — is your sister really that unreasonable, or is this more about *your* shit than hers? Uh huh.

- **If you *do know* the consequences of saying no, are they WORSE than whatever happens if you say yes?**

Are we talking "someone might be annoyed with you," "someone might yell at you," or "someone might fire/disown you" if you say no? Because at least one, if not two of those are better than a lot of potential consequences of saying yes to X, depending on what X is and how badly you don't want to do it.

It's up to you to weigh the pros and cons — and make sure they are *true* pros and cons, not merely the Yes-Men talking. **Then, take a calculated risk.** If saying yes will enable a reward greater than your sacrifice would cost, that's awesome. But "I'm just hardwired to be an overachiever!" is not a good reason to do everything everyone ever asks you to do. Please trust me on this.

In sum: if you establish that you probably **SHOULD** or definitely

HAVE TO say yes to X in order to accomplish something else — like keeping the peace with family or keeping your boss happy so you can keep your job so you can keep your paycheck so you can keep your apartment — then suck it up and say yes. We've all got problems.

(Seriously, there's **no point in wasting more time, energy, and money** dawdling over the injustice of life's shitty little necessities. **Spend the fuck bucks** *doing,* **not resenting.**)

But if you run through the preceding questions and you realize no is a reasonable and realistic response — as well as a risk you're willing to take — that, we can work with.

Take a spin through the flowchart on the next page, and refer back to it liberally—both as you read *Fuck No!* and as you're sitting in your cubicle mulling your coworker's latest request to impose on your goodwill. Do you really *have* to?

You decide.

Alright, chickens, now that we've gotten a handle on your hang-ups, let's get to work on **managing your mind-set — and changing it from Yes-Man to** *No, Ma'am!*

Remember when I said that you need to stop thinking of saying no as "too hard"? I'm going to show you **how** *I* **learned to flip that mental script** and think of saying no as ultimately MUCH easier than giving in and saying yes.

People-Pleasers and Pushovers: this one's for you.

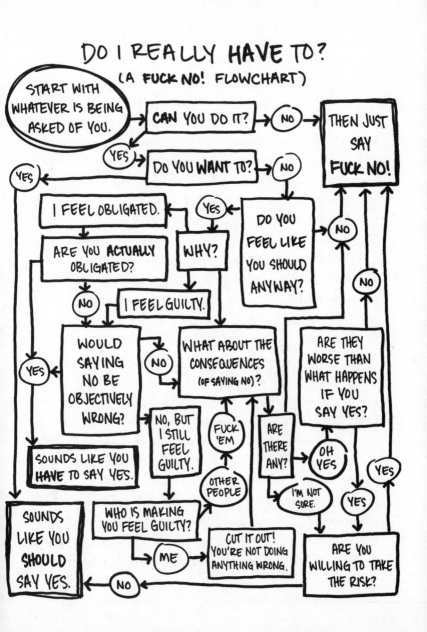

Easy come, easy no

As you may have gleaned from earlier foreshadowing, I once agreed to host a baby shower despite the fact that babies are emphatically not my scene. I did this because my very pregnant friend suggested it, and I couldn't immediately think of a way to scuttle the idea without hurting her feelings or looking like the baby-hating bitch that, to be fair, I totally am.

Instead, I blurted out a yes, hoped for the best, and got plannin'. With the mom-to-be's approval, I settled on a Baby Boy Bourbon and BBQ theme at a reasonable hour of the evening. (Teetotal noontime parties: also not my scene.)

A few weeks went by. My friend got more and more pregnant. I ordered favors and decorations and set the guest list and finalized a menu. And then — SURPRISE! — another friend of my friend offered to host her baby shower without knowing one was already in the works. At which point my friend, perhaps exhibiting her own inability to say no lest she hurt someone's feelings, said something more like "Sure! How about you and Sarah co-host it!"

And lo, **many of my plans were un-planned**. I went from the convenience of setting up in my own apartment to schlepping supplies to somebody else's and from evening adult gathering to afternoon diaper decorating faster than you can sever an umbilical cord. (I did distribute the gingham-checked takeout containers full of blue M&Ms and Bourbon nips that I'd already ordered, but only because consuming all of them myself right before the party would have been unseemly.)

Was it a lovely little fiesta? Absolutely! **But in what world was it easier for me to have co-hosted it than to have nodded and smiled, said, "I must confess, I don't think I'm your gal for that," and gone on about my day?**

The answer is no world. In no world would this have been the case.

In fact, when I look back on it, mama was probably just throwing out an idle suggestion that she never expected me to say yes to. She knew me better than that. I wish I had known me better than that.

Anyway, lesson learned.

Ever since, when I'm faced with something I don't want to do but it feels too hard to say no, **I invoke Baby Shower 2010 as a sort of talisman.** I pause. I recall how things worked out for me in that situation, and it helps me shift my internal response to this latest proposition from *Uh, okay I guess I can do this it won't be so bad I'll figure it out later* to *Oh no, no no no this shit has got to be nipped in the* motherfucking bud *right now.*

I'm guessing you've had a similar experience, no? Maybe a few, but no need to overachieve. **Pick one for now and write it down here:**

_____

_____

What did it cost you (physically, emotionally, and/or financially)? Write that down too:

_____

_____

_____

In hindsight, do you agree that it would have been easier to say

no in the first place? Yeah. I thought so. And as the great philosopher, poet, and novelist George Santayana once said: "Those who cannot remember the past are condemned to repeat it."*

You've got to take that hindsight and make it work for you in the future, Marty McFly styles.

Choose your own talisman. Meditate on it. And when the need arises, **use it like a mental shortcut to reroute your brain from NO = TOO HARD to NO = ACTUALLY MUCH EASIER.**

The more you practice, the more it'll become second nature to **think about the consequences of saying yes** before you take the action of saying no.

And when you *do* take that action?

Don't be rude, dude.

How to say what you really mean without being really mean

You don't have to be nasty when saying no. You *can* do it that way, but you shouldn't. If you're out there making enemies and hurting people's feelings with your particular brand of naysaying, you're ruining it for the rest of us.

---

* I'm not going to pretend I knew who George Santayana was before I Googled that quote. I thought it came from Churchill but when I went to confirm, I found out he stole and paraphrased it like forty years later. What a guy.

If you've read *The Life-Changing Magic of Not Giving a Fuck,* then you've heard this song before. Forgive me, for whenever possible I do aim to provide original content, but there's a reason that book hit a nerve — and a big part of its appeal lies in learning how to give fewer fucks **without *also* turning into an asshole**, a core philosophy that bears repeating.

Hey, if it ain't broke, don't nix it.

Instead, pretty please practice **HONESTY and POLITENESS (H&P)** when you have, say, a book club invite from Janet that you wish to decline. And note that **H&P are not absolutes, but rather two axes of a grid within which your ideal response will rest.** You can go with the flow and get down on the let down in whatever way makes the most sense for your situation.

- **If a scheduling conflict means you really can't be there, this works:**

    "I can't make it, but have fun!"
    (Totally honest and extra polite.)

- **If you have a conflict, but you're not exactly *sad* about this fact:**

    "Unfortunately, I'm not available."
    (It's true that Janet will find your RSVP status unfortunate even if you don't. And you're polite enough to keep things ambiguous.)

- **If the one and only reason you don't want to join Janet's book club is because you hate her stupid face, then being *completely honest* would in and of itself be *extremely rude*. In such cases, omit the TMI and/or fib slightly for the greater good:**

  "Tuesday at seven? Ah, no, I can't go. But I appreciate you including me."

  (Your decline has nothing to do with the specific timing of "Chapters & Chardonnay" and everything to do with the fact that spending three hours in close proximity to Janet, *ever*, makes you want to gag on that cheap white she favors, so I call this one SOMEWHAT MISLEADING but STILL POLITE.)

  "No, I don't have time."

  (A bit curt? Yes. A lie of omission? Perhaps. But leaving "for your stupid face" off the end of that sentence is in everyone's best interests.)

I'll give you more examples of elegant execution as we move along, but that's the gist on theory. Be honest, be polite, or be a combination of the two that gets the job done without sending Janet sobbing into her copy of *Eat, Pray, Love*.

You're better than that.

Sorry, NotSorry

While we're on the topic of honesty, politeness, and me repeating myself, when I was writing my first book I invented the **NotSorry**

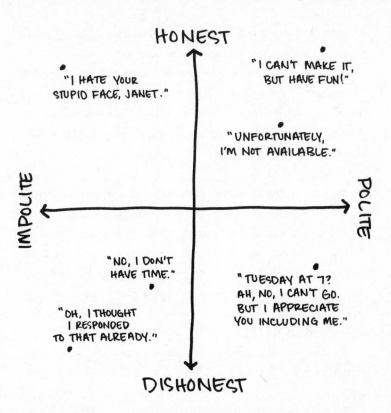

HONEST

"I HATE YOUR
STUPID FACE, JANET."

"I CAN'T MAKE IT,
BUT HAVE FUN!"

"UNFORTUNATELY,
I'M NOT AVAILABLE."

IMPOLITE ← → POLITE

"NO, I DON'T
HAVE TIME."

"TUESDAY AT 7?
AH, NO, I CAN'T GO.
BUT I APPRECIATE
YOU INCLUDING ME."

"OH, I THOUGHT
I RESPONDED
TO THAT ALREADY."

DISHONEST

Method, a two-step strategy for figuring out what you don't give a fuck (i.e., care) *about* and then no longer giving your fucks (in the form of your time, energy, and money) *to* those things. SPOILER ALERT: it's just more mental decluttering, but this method's kicky name comes from how you feel when you've successfully completed it, using—you guessed it—honesty and politeness to make your decision and carry it out. **You've done nothing wrong, so you have nothing to feel guilty about: you are "not sorry."***

When it comes to not giving a fuck, I stand by NotSorry a million percent. However, you will notice that throughout *this* book, **I often suggest throwing an "I'm sorry" into the mix when delivering your no.** That's not because I think you should feel guilty about your response. It's purely procedural.

How so?

Because **saying an *active* no to something is more than just *passively* not giving a fuck (i.e., not caring) about that thing.**

If you don't give a fuck about, say, Iceland, you also don't have to work up the balls to say no *to* Iceland. Iceland will never know if you decide not to set foot in its steamy, mineral-rich lagoons. You're off the hook! Whereas other situations will require clear written or verbal no's, the likes of which I'm here to help you compose HONESTLY AND POLITELY.

So with regard to saying — if not always *being* — sorry, here's my two *krónur*:

- Sometimes you will care quite a bit about the person, thing, or opportunity that you still *can't* or *shouldn't* say yes to. You ARE sorry! Might as well be honest about it.
- Even if you don't really care, apologizing is like lube; it reduces friction and makes things easier and more pleasant for both

---

* Much like I'm #NotSorry about exploiting a popular extant hashtag for my own personal gain.

parties. Be polite, take the high road, and express your regrets. (Careful though, the high road is slippery.)

- If you find feigning sincerity a bit of a drag, think of your "Sorry" as applicable to a different aspect of your no than the recipient might presume. Like maybe you're not actually sorry that you can't blow zillions of dollars and most of your self-respect going to your friends' vow-renewal ceremony at Coachella, but you *are* sorry that saying no means you may never see what Justin Bieber's abs look like in person. Same difference.

Thanks so much!

"Thanks" or iterations thereof (e.g., "I really appreciate it" or "It's so kind of you to think of me") may not appear in each and every sample response throughout *Fuck No!*, but that's because I'm trying to keep it spicy and also I shouldn't have to tell you to say thank you every time the opportunity arises. Who raised you? A little gratitude goes a long way toward maintaining friendships and mollifying moms who were really hoping you'd be available to be the fourth for bridge this week with the girls. *Oh, thanks so much for asking, but I've got something that night. Hi to Dad!*

With all of the preceding No Theory in mind, we're inching ever closer to **unleashing your skills on other people** in part II: How to say no to pretty much anything.

Are you nervous?

Don't be!

I understand that **for *no*-vices such as yourself, saying no to**

those you care about or on whom you depend to make a living might still seem daunting. So before we go full-tilt boogie on moms, dads, sisters, brothers, bosses, and besties, I'm going to lob out a few softballs to get your head in the game.

From proselytizers to small-talkers to bartenders, salespeople, and neighbors, we'll practice polite but firm declines on those to whom you can say *nei** without ruining valued relationships or disrupting any delicate power dynamics.

I shall call them **scenari-nos,** because I cannot resist even a mediocre pun.

Scenari-nos: a practice round

We'll begin by setting our sights on a real easy target: **people you don't even like.** For example:

- **High school acquaintances you weren't that fond of back in the day**

You do not have to have coffee with these folks just because you had the bad luck to run into them in the wrapping paper aisle at Target when you were home visiting your parents for Christmas. You can always hand out your phone number with one "accidental" incorrect digit, but that's child's play. Instead, when Rick-who-peaked-in-JV-basketball asks, you could answer:

---

* Norwegian optional

"Thanks, but I'm pretty busy this week."

"I'm not in town for long. Maybe next time!"

HEY, LOOK WHAT YOU DID. You set a boundary (i.e., decided what you're willing and not willing to do) and you enforced it (i.e., said no to Rick). **You protected your time, energy, and money.** Your sheep would thank you, if sheep could talk.

You can do the same in the face of anyone you don't like: **other parents from your kid's school; ex-girlfriends; annoying fellow gym-goers; even, I daresay, professional contacts who rub you so indisputably the wrong way, they might as well be sand in your panties.** (Not the ones you're forced to deal with to get your job done, but those nonessential players you merely feel like you "should" be meeting for lunch or chatting up at industry events. The only thing you "should" be doing in situations like these is saying, "Sorry, I'm booked up for the foreseeable future.")

No-Tip: Get proactive! You don't have to wait for the question to get asked, the invitation to get issued, or the meeting to get scheduled. Instead, you can issue a **Proactive No**, making it clear ahead of time that you're not available. This could be as easy as throwing down a personal policy against "breakfast dates" before a colleague can suggest one, or speed-walking right past Rick while miming "I really need to find the bathroom!" Other times, a Proactive No involves anticipating the question, raising it *yourself*, and then answering it all in one fell swoop (see pages 124 and 213). Damn, you're good.

∗ ∗ ∗

This doesn't seem so hard, does it?

I hope not, because the entire thesis of this book is that "saying no doesn't have to be so fucking hard" and I do like to deliver on expectations.

Now, how about saying *jo** to **people you don't even *know?***

● **Small talk**

My husband chats up strangers while waiting for drinks at the bar. My stepmother-in-law makes friends on airplanes. Unlike them (but much like a contestant on *The Bachelor*), I'm not here to make friends — in line, online, or otherwise. Sometimes I do it anyway, because I have had three vodka tonics. But usually I shut down unwanted small talk with a look that once caused my friend Sylvie to say "Wow. *Respect.*"

(To be fair, the small talkers in question were Trump supporters from Florida and I did not move all the way to the Dominican Republic to put up with that shit at my local dive bar.)

This look, should you wish to attempt it, consists of five steps:

Step 1: Make eye contact with the small talkers.

Step 2: Squint as though you can't see them very well.

Step 3: Smirk ever so slightly.

Step 4: Say "Mmmmm" and nod real slow.

Step 5: Swivel away.

---

* In Albanian, if you're so inclined.

Works every time.

Next we have **people you may or may not like, and may or may not know very well, but regardless, sometimes interacting with them is unavoidable.** Such as:

- **Neighbors**

Waking hours are waking hours. We all know we shouldn't be leaf-blowing at 6 a.m. on a suburban Saturday or hosting midnight stilt-walking classes in a top-floor unit.

That said, you don't deserve to be admonished for living in a manner that — while objectionable to your neighbor — is not *objectively* wrong, bad, or disrespectful. Or that was accidental and won't be repeated if the Paw Patrol could take two seconds to approach you like an adult instead of posting photos of your puppy's lawn biscuits on the neighborhood association chatroom and calling for your head on a poo-poo platter.

But it's not just complaints; you're also bound to get a few well-intentioned requests from neighbors over time, not all of which you can, should, or want to accede to. Below are a few familiar strains of each, and what you might say in response if you believe them to be unfounded or untenable.

WHAT'S THAT YOU SAY, MRS. ROBINSON?

REQUEST	RESPONSE
"Can you make your baby stop crying?"	I'm afraid that's not how babies work, but I do apologize for the noise."
"We're having a party. Can we use your driveway for parking?"	"Sorry, but no. Last time too many of your guests passed out naked in your backyard and left us parked in."
"I can hear you typing. Can you move your desk into the closet?"	"That's not a feasible arrangement, but I have a pair of old earmuffs I'm not using, if you think they'd help muffle the sound."
"I find your rainbow flags offensive to my faith. Must you put them in every single window?"	"Every window? Probably not. But you don't need seven Pence 2020 signs on your lawn either, so I guess we're even."
"Can I borrow your drill?"	"No, but only because you never gave it back to me last time, so you already have it."
"Have you ever considered leaving your curtains open at night?"	"Get away from me, you creep."

It feels like you're starting to get the hang of this! Let's nibble some more low-hanging fruit in the form of **unsolicited calls, offers, and entreaties.**

● Telemarketers

If you find yourself on the receiving end of an unsolicited call from someone attempting to part you with your money in exchange for goods or services you are not seeking, it is acceptable to hang up. You didn't ask for this call; you don't have to take it. Some people may think hanging up on a telemarketer is rude, but I think it exists in a gray area that you may enter and luxuriate in like your own personal rooftop Jacuzzi.

Anything short of a dial tone is catnip to these charmers, who are armed with *entire scripts* to prevent you from hanging up no matter what words you use when trying to politely decline to partake in their goods or services.

For example if you say "Not today, thanks" they will respond "Ah, but this is a one-time only offer — are you sure you want to pass it up?" (FOMO: activated!) And if you say "Honestly, I'm not interested" they'll come back with "I've heard that before, sir, but if you'll allow me a moment to explain further, I think you'll change your mind." (Still listening? Pushover.)

If you don't put an end to it pronto, this pushy pas de deux will continue until your defenses are worn to nubs, and in six to eight business days you're the owner of a discount wind turbine that makes your yard look like a futuristic yet low-budget mini-golf course.

Just. Hang. Up.

Or—and this is what I do—screen your fucking calls and don't pick up in the first place. **Power No. BOOM.**

No-Tip: File under "never gonna read it." I hope it goes without saying that if you receive an unsolicited email or snail mail solicitation for anything that you don't want to buy, sponsor, or subscribe to, you can just hit DELETE or toss it in the circular file and never think about it again. Not even once. Seriously, it's okay.

● **Free shit**

Some people looooooove free shit. Furniture, electronics, old canoes—you name it, they'll take it off your hands. That's great for them, and for Series A investors in Craigslist. But YOU do not have to say yes to free shit just because a person wants to give it to you. If you say no, they will find someone else to pawn it off on; or leave it on the curb to make a broke kid's lucky day; or take it to the Salvation Army or the dump; or keep it for themselves, which they may have secretly wanted to do the whole time.

Being a compulsive tidier, I've been known to give away lots of stuff. When we moved to the Dominican Republic, our old neighbors Matt and Liz came into a gloriously complete collection of Crate & Barrel glassware. Red wine, white wine, champagne, martini—you name it. We're talking *pilsner* glasses here, people!

But although I'm delighted when friends or strangers are inclined to accept my free shit, I also don't mind if they say no. It's their prerogative. Ergo, if anyone (including me) offers you clothes or tools or housewares or canoes you don't want, please don't hesitate to reference this page in your reply:

"Hmm, it's not really my style. Maybe [a friend whose style matches better with this item] might want it?"

"I wouldn't have anywhere to hang a ten-foot-long latch hook version of *The Last Supper*, but thanks."

"I appreciate the offer, but I don't think I need an as-seen-on-TV stencil toaster."

"I already have one." Or "How funny, I just got rid of one of those too!"*

No-Tip: I'll have to think about that. Saying no in person, in the moment, can be tricky. There's not much time to ask Why Yes/When No when you're standing toe-to-toe with a fellow human who's intent on eliciting a response. I promise that with practice, it'll get easier: "The no-ment of truth"), but in the meantime, master the phrase, "I'll have to think about that." It's a polite, natural way to press PAUSE on the conversation until you're ready to resume — be that in two minutes, two days, or two weeks from never.

- **Those who wish to convert you to their religion**

I'm not keen on being exhorted to join anyone's flock, especially if the pitch entails harassing me on the street or showing up at my home

---

* LIAR. You *lie*.

uninvited. The latter happened not infrequently in the small town I grew up in, and one day, I actually answered the door to strangers and shouted "We don't want any!" before shutting it triumphantly in their faces and sashaying back to the living room and my parents' bewilderment. My father got up to investigate and it turned out to be a family whose ancestors had once owned our house and who just wanted to see it while they were passing through. I let Dad field that one while I died of embarrassment behind the couch. Oops. Little too quick on the pshaw, there, Sarah.

But hey, I can learn from my mistakes and so can you! There are more polite ways to turn away unexpected visitors, be they or be they not children of God.

First, figure out what the door-knockers want. If it's your neighbor hoping to borrow your drill, we went over this already (see page 72). If they're strangers soliciting for donations or signatures, don't worry, we'll get there. And if they really are Jesus freaks, and you are not freaky for Jesus, see below:

"Not for me, thanks."

"I'm not really into organized religion, but you do you."

"You're barking up the wrong crucifix. Have a good day."

OPTIONAL POWER NO:
Do not get up. Do not pass Go. Do not answer the door. (Or do answer it, but in a Santa hat, a jingle bell collar, and nothing else.)

- **Shots**

I'm talking alcohol here, not vaccinations. You should definitely get vaccinated, and both I and my fragile grasp on herd immunity are willing to get hate mail for saying that. But if a bartender is pushing two-ounce vials of loony juice that you do not wish to imbibe, one of the below responses should get you off the hook.

"I don't want one."

"Nah, someone else can have it."

"I have a personal policy against doing shots."

Or you can perfect a move that my husband used at a bachelor party a few years ago, which involves accepting the shot and then angling your body such that your shot-taking hand is hidden from others' view by your face, and when you all knock back your Jägers at the same time, yours goes over your shoulder and onto the floor instead of burning a trail to your bloodstream. Not coincidentally, it is easier to succeed at this maneuver if you are more sober than the people around you.

● **Fundraising calls (see also: donations, loans, and investments, page 141)**

I once spent a few evenings participating in a fundraising drive for Harvard. It was a job that paid undergrads like me a meager hourly wage to dial down a list of alumni who had pledged to donate to the university and deliver them a friendly reminder that today might just be the day to make good.

To be honest, I felt a little gross about it, but also: there were cookies.

Our lists were divided by the donors' graduating classes so that we could casually mention on the call if there was a big anniversary coming up like a fiftieth reunion, or say, "Oh, do you know so-and-so who was also class of '88?" Make it personal, keep 'em talking, get the credit card number while you're at it.

Eventually, I realized why the other students who'd done this before took the lists of the more recent graduates and left the classes of 1950 and further back to newbies like me. Initially, I thought I'd have more success with older alums who'd had time to amass their fortunes, rather than a bunch of twenty- to forty-somethings still saddled with the kind of student loan debt I myself would be paying off for the next twelve years. But then a nice older woman answered, and when I explained that I was calling about her husband's pledge to donate to his alma mater, she informed me that he would not be donating... because he had died recently.

Like, *very* recently.

Like, yesterday.

Fuck.

Which is to say, I understand that fundraising is a shitty job and that someone has to do it. Universities, political campaigns, medical research, saving a whole species or a single local landmark that's about to get torn down: for the organizations asking for your money, these are noble, essential causes; for you, they may seem less so. Either way, you could be talking to a paid staffer or just an unpaid volunteer or a poor college student or the intern who drew the short straw. It doesn't hurt the pandas for you to be polite.

"I appreciate what you're doing, but I can't donate today."

"This isn't a great time for me. Have a nice day."

"I'm not interested, but good luck to you."

OPTIONAL ACCEPTABLE FIB:
Profit once more from my faux pas and say that the person your unsolicited caller is looking for died recently. What are they gonna do, Google it? No, they're gonna hang up, eat another cookie, and move on down the list.

Next up: **semi-solicited offers.** You put yourself out there for selling — and upselling — because you walked into a store or sat down at a restaurant, but you still have the right to say *le** to more than you want or less than you need.

● **Can I help you find something?**

Be they salespeople at the H&M you only stepped into for the air conditioning or the dude trying to sell you a parrot on the beach in Rio de Janeiro, vendors are just pitching product, and you're allowed to pass. Same goes for any street-corner or subway-platform seller-of-wares. (I say this as a woman living in the Dominican Republic who has more than once rebuffed a chap selling *fresh mozzarella cheese* off of the handlebars of his motorbike.)

If you're trying to relax on your vacation or get from the bus stop to your office without purchasing a rayon skirt, a live tropical bird, or a knockoff DVD of the new live-action *Aladdin,* you can be polite but firm in the following manner:

"No, I'm just browsing."

"I'm all set, thanks."

"Sorry, I'm in a hurry!" (Not ideal if you're currently lying supine on a beach towel, obvs.)

---

* Works best if you're in Malta, since that is Maltese for "no."

"I'm allergic to birds."

"Not a big Will Smith fan, to be honest."

No-tip: Not so fast! If your hairdresser suggests a radical cut or color or shaping of sideburns, it's okay to say "Not today, thanks. I'd need more time to get used to that idea." On one hand, they see a lot of hair on a daily basis and undoubtedly have some idea of what would look good on you. On the other hand, Cersei Lannister *died* before she was able to grow out that pixie cut. Cautionary tale.

● **Would you like fries with that?**

Let it be known that I do not have anything against upselling as a concept. I appreciate being informed that there are four more colors of that tank top waiting for me on the rack around the corner, and that if I buy the eight-ounce version of my favorite lotion instead of the six, I'll unlock 10 percent off on my next purchase. Get it, Bath & Body Works.*

I also respect that waitstaff are trained to tempt you with appetizers, desserts, and better bottles of booze because it juices the check and, appropriately, their tip. Same with stylists who make commission moving high-end pomade and badger-hair brushes, and realtors who push your stated spending limit because they have the *perfect* two-bed with outdoor space just *slightly out of your range*. And as for vets urging expensive house-made chow on gullible pet owners as

---

* By the way, did you know there are several more hilarious, profane, self-help manuals in the series? http://nofucksgivenguides.com/the-books/

though animals don't eat their own feces on a regular basis and live to tell the tale? Well played.

But all's fair in no and war. **You're allowed to decline the upgrade or additional service.**

I haven't always been mindful of this type of thing. For example, my doctor's office in New York used to run a side biz trying to unload supplements on patients at the checkout desk, and I'm ashamed to say a $45 bottle of Bone Builder followed me to two different apartments over the course of five years before I finally threw it away and admitted defeat.

I never made that mistake again, but unfortunately **"buyer's remorse" only becomes a future deterrent** *after* **you've bought something.** Instead, save yourself the down payment with an upfront no, girding yourself and your wallet with the following truths:

---

6 ways to say no to someone who's trying to upsell you

"I'm good!"
"I'm going to stick with my first choice."
"Nah."
"Tempting, but no."
"I really need to stay on budget."
"No thanks!"

People who are trying to sell you shit are used to hearing no. They won't take it personally, and if they do, they shouldn't be working in sales. Not your problem.

You will not be the first to say no to a hawker of extras and you will not be the last. If you also don't want to be the one cluttering your home, office, car, or digestive system with junk you don't need, take heed.

Saying no is free. Organic protein shakes for your cat are not.

● **Sorry, is that okay?**

Not a sales tactic, *per se,* but a question that gets posed with some regularity by people whom you're paying for goods and services, and to whom you probably answer yes rather often when you really want to say, "NO. NO IT FUCKING ISN'T."

Let's say you're at a restaurant and because you are a responsible customer who doesn't assume a kitchen can just provide whatever you happen to be in the mood for that day, you read the menu. Good work. You settle on your order — again, straight off the menu — but a few details remain unclear. For example, the menu says "cola" or "mustard" but doesn't specify which *kind* of each. So when you relay your order to the waiter, you say exactly what you want — Diet Coke and Dijon. At which point the waiter tells you actually they serve only Pepsi products and yellow mustard:

"Sorry, is that okay?"

If you *can't, shouldn't,* or *don't want to* accept the substitute, then YOU DO NOT HAVE TO SAY YES.

This is not a complicated concept, and yet many of us get all tongue-tied and people-pleasey and say yes and wind up **ordering and paying for things we didn't want and don't like.** WTF? Instead, just say "Thanks for letting me know, in that case I'll have an iced tea." Or "Yellow mustard is an abomination. Glad I asked!" and proceed to receive a satisfactory beverage and a turkey sandwich unmolested by inferior condiments.

But wait. There's more…

What if you specify "Diet Coke" when you order and the waiter *doesn't mention* that this is not the cola they stock, and just brings you a Diet Pepsi and you gag on your first sip and have to ask "Wait, is this Diet Pepsi?" and they say "Yeah, we don't have Diet Coke. Sorry, is that okay?"

YOU ARE ALLOWED TO SAY NO HERE TOO. What a world we live in!

With the exception of food allergies that could potentially land you in the ICU, the waiter does not even need to know your reasons, nor, I'm certain, do they care. Any of the following are acceptable responses:

"I actually don't like [substitute] and would prefer to get something else if that's okay." (It is.)

"Hmm, I thought so. I really don't want this. Can you please take it back?" (They can.)

"Gotcha. Unfortunately, if I'd known that I wouldn't have ordered it. Can you take it off my bill?" (And so they shall.)

God, Pepsi is disgusting. But the broader lesson here — beyond simple menu substitutions — is **that if someone offers you something you don't want or does something to you that you don't like and then says "Sorry, is that okay?" you don't have to take it, literally or figuratively.** (This rule applies to everyone, not just service professionals. Such as the roommate who borrowed your brand-new latex dress before you ever had a chance to wear it and stretched it out because she has six inches and twenty pounds on you. NOT OKAY.)

What *is* okay is to honestly and politely express your disappointment, displeasure, or disagreement so that whatever it is doesn't happen again — to you or to future victims of the Brooklyn manicurist I used to refer to as the Butcher of Waverly Avenue.

NO, ACTUALLY, IT'S NOT OKAY.

Massage therapist	"Thanks for asking. That was too hard. Can you hold back a little?"
Bartender	"Ah, I've never seen a martini garnished with cilantro. Maybe we could try this again. Perhaps with…mmm…I don't know. An olive?"
Mechanic	"You accidentally erased all my radio presets? No, dude. The only thing that would make that okay is a ten percent discount. How 'bout it?"
Hotel desk clerk	"Yeah…if I wanted to spend my vacation inside a nicely wallpapered ashtray, I would have ordered a smoking room. Since I do not and did not, I'm going to have to ask you to move me. A free upgrade is also acceptable. Thanks!"
Manicurist	"Ouch, that hurt. Please be more careful."

Incidentally, the preceding advice is pertinent to **your personal okay-ness,** too.

If I may speak earnestly for a moment (not my usual M.O., so bear with me), it seems like a lot of us have an impulse to brush people off when they ask **"Hey, are you doing okay?"** We say "Yeah, I'm fine" — even when it's abundantly clear from our disheveled appearance or disgruntled mien that we are not.

Maybe we lie because we don't feel like getting into the reasons why we're not actually okay. Or because we aren't sure the person asking truly wants to know those reasons.

Whatever the case, I used to do that a lot myself.

But then a couple of years ago I had Very Bad Day, during which I a) had a gynecologist appointment, b) took a train headed in the wrong direction, c) arrived very late, sweaty, and anxious to my doctor's office, and d) discovered that I had the date wrong and my appointment was the next day, meaning e) I would have to deal with both the journey and the anticipation of having my cervix scraped all over again tomorrow.

I exited my ob-gyn's building in what you might politely call a "state" and wandered down the street into a Victoria's Secret, seeking the tried-and-true balm of retail therapy for my woes. In retrospect, I don't know what part of "Get naked and stare at your anxious, sweaty corpus in a starkly lit dressing room mirror" I thought was going to make me feel *better* in that moment, but anyway.

I ended up in the fitting rooms, where a young saleswoman asked me if I was okay. Instead of my usual polite nod and skedaddle away from approaching merchants, this time I said **"You know what? No. I'm not having such a great day, to be honest."**

She nodded. "Yeah, I could tell by your face. Come on, we're going to help you out."

In that moment, I felt seen — in my bad way, and in a good way. A little bit of my burden was lifted. At last, things were looking up.

So the moral of this story is that if you're not okay — and someone calls you out on it and your instinct is to be all "Yeah, I'm fine" — maybe instead you should tell the truth? Just say "No. I'm not okay." If that opens some floodgates, more power to you, but you can also stick with "And I don't really want to talk about it, but thanks for asking."

I think you'll get some relief. And who knows? You might even discover you've been wearing the wrong size bra your whole life and emerge from that conversation a new woman.

Frankly, I think we should all get more comfortable saying/ shouting "No, I am not fucking okay!" — not just on Very Bad Days, but when we do things like fall off a bike or take a baseball to the crotch or randomly trip on a patch of grass in the park and faceplant in front of a bunch of strangers. It's cathartic. Other cathartic things to say/shout in those moments include:

"Holy mother of Christ, that hurt."

"DO I *LOOK* OKAY, SUSAN?"

"Why are you people standing around gaping when at least one of you could be getting me an ice pack and a cocktail?!"

And that's a wrap on our practice round. Woot! Soon, I'll be upping the ante to **those you quite like, or even love,** as well as **those who hold your fate (and sometimes, your paychecks) in their hands.** But before we get there, I want to take one teensy little detour to examine a surprisingly common thread from my survey.

After all of my nosy questions about specific subsets of humans to whom we all want and need to say no, I asked, **"Is there anyone else in your life you wish you could say no to?"**

And a bunch of people responded: Me.*

Me, myself, and I

Some of my respondents were talking about **willpower.** They wished they could say no to the voice in their own heads when they *wanted* to eat a jelly donut, but also felt they *shouldn't,* because it would ruin their dinner or disrupt their blood-sugar levels.

Others were talking about **battling their inner demons,** like the perfectionist who *wanted* to keep tinkering with a project even when they knew they *must* finish it ASAP. Or the person trying and failing to suffocate the FOMO that causes them to RSVP yes to everything even though it's clear they *can't* do it all.

Well, if they (and you) have been paying attention—which I'm sure you all have, because you're awesome—then by now everyone ought to realize that **it makes no difference** if you're directing your

---

* Not "me" as in yours truly, although I'm sure my husband took the survey and he probably does wish that from time to time. But "me" as in *themselves.*

decline at other people who would wrongfully deplete your Fuck Budget or putting the kibosh on bad habits and behaviors of your own.

YOU set your boundaries.

YOU enforce them.

As the cherry on top of our practice round, let's take an example that's near and dear to my own people-pleasing, overachieving heart:

- **Planning and organizing shit**

Is it flattering that friends and family think of you when it's time to concoct a rockin' party, devise an enviable vacation, or map out a road trip that would give Thelma and Louise a run for their money? Does it make sense that former classmates would tap the person who handled the bake sales and raffles and prom prep twenty-five years ago as the logical person to plan the reunion next summer?

Yup. They all know you're creative and organized and reliable.

Plus, you always say yes to this stuff. They know that too.

I know . . . it's just . . . I'm so good at it!

Yes, well, JUST BECAUSE YOU ALWAYS DO EVERYTHING WELL AND PROPERLY DOESN'T MEAN YOU SHOULD GET STUCK DOING IT FOR EVERYONE ELSE, ALL THE TIME.

Next time you get asked to herd the cats or play concierge, **do you, yourself, and you a favor:** plumb the depths of your Fuck Budget, recognize its limits, set some boundaries (say no TO yourself), and enforce them (say no FOR yourself).

Then, instead of your usual automatic yes, supply one of these all-purpose replies:

"Thanks so much for asking, but I'm good with whatever everybody else comes up with. I don't need to be in charge here."

"This is going to be such a blast, I confess I'd rather enjoy it purely as a guest, not a host."

"Oof, I pulled a planning muscle last month and it's still sore. I'm going to sit this one out."

Got it? **"No" always begins with you.** It begins with asking yourself questions about the situation at hand —

Can I?

Must I?

Should I?

Will I?

— and answering them honestly:

I can't.

I don't have to.

I shouldn't.

I won't.

You've got to — as one of my survey-takers so brilliantly put it — **"hit your own 'nuff button."** If you can't set boundaries and enforce them for *yourself*, you'll never be able to say no to anything else — including an inanimate pastry, a perfectionist streak, or the Evite for opening night at that new molecular gastronomy joint whose email list you somehow ended up on and that wouldn't be your thing even if you weren't already triple-booked on Saturday night.

A donut cannot force you to eat it. **You have all the power in this relationship.**

A presentation does not demand that you re-jigger every slide in a slightly more attractive font. **You decide if that is truly a good use of your time.**

A restaurant will not fail because you didn't have the time, energy, or wherewithal to eat a ludicrously priced ramekin of celery foam this weekend. **You can just click NO.**

This is why they call it *self*-control, *self*-improvement, and *self*-help. Hey, I don't make the rules. I just make the flowcharts.

The joy of no

Before we move on to part II, I want to introduce one last, potentially less obvious but no less rewarding outcome of your new life of

No, Not now, and *Never again* — which is that **when YOU learn how to say no and stick to it, it's a positive development for EVERYONE.**

Yes, you'll be happier when you're getting more of the good stuff and less of the bad stuff out of life — where good stuff equals freedom, an afternoon to yourself, and a balance in your bank account instead of on your credit card, and bad stuff equals untenable deadlines, unwanted advances, and those freaky little anchovy fillets they insist on depositing atop an otherwise yummy Caesar salad.

And you being happier is my number one priority here. But if you play your cards right, I'm telling you that *other people will be happier too.*

Your friends? Instead of hemming, hawing, and leaving them hanging, you'll be letting them down quickly and gently. They'll appreciate it! I mean, wouldn't you?

Your family? Instead of doing things with and for them under duress, stoking the fires of resentment and creating the wrong kind of memories, you'll be preserving the quality of the time you *do* spend together.

Your bosses, clients, and colleagues? Instead of overcommitting and potentially under-delivering, you'll be setting manageable expectations that prevent them from getting burned when your circuits overload.

By God, I love the people I can depend on to respond swiftly to invitations, *especially* if it's a no. Helping me plan ahead shows me that you care — much more so than showing up out of guilt or a sense of obligation and not enjoying yourself because you never wanted to be there in the first place.

Honestly expressing that you can't do me a favor is a favor in and of itself. Now I have time to ask someone else. Or not, if you saying no has made me realize I shouldn't have bothered you or anyone with it in the first place. Way to pay it forward, pal!

And being clear and uncompromising about your ability or desire to meet a deadline or accomplish a task makes me positively giddy inside. YOU ARE EXACTLY THE KIND OF PERSON I WANT ON MY TEAM.

Yup. Learning to say no in the right way, at the right time, with the right words (and attitude and facial expressions and select hand gestures) can improve your relationships and make all of your interactions more fun and fruitful.

That's **the joy of no.** And as with cooking and sex, there are just as many recipes and positions to get you there.

Part II is where the magic happens.

11

BECOMING A NO-IT-ALL:
How to say no to pretty much anything

Now that you've granted yourself permission to say no, the rest of the book is chock full of all the ammunition you'll ever need to do so.

We'll cover **invitations**, from dinner parties to weddings to joining the club; **favors** (requests *and* offers); **asking permission and withholding consent; professional inquiries, demands, and negotiations**; and reckoning with **romantic partners**. Along the way, I'll serve up sample no's for friends, dates, bosses, Blue Men, and more.

Then, because things tend to get more complicated when it comes to those with whom you share genetic material (or even just a last name and a Verizon plan), **family gets a dedicated chapter.** I'll roll out an extensive collection of **niche negatories for parents, siblings, children, aunts, uncles, cousins, and anyone else to whom you're linked by blood, marriage, adoption,** or because you have one of those families where you call your dad's friend Uncle Bill even though he's not really your uncle.

Got **in-laws?** Got 'em covered.

Throughout part II I'll drop a bit more No Theory; unleash several **amusing and instructive personal anecdotes**; and help you build a strong and steady foundation to **decline, refuse, turn down, pass up, and opt-out of anything your little heart desires.**

Or doesn't desire, as the case may be.

So what are you waiting for?

Let's no!

INVITATIONS

fancy fêtes, informal gatherings, opening nights, shamanic rituals, and joining the club

Gather 'round, boys and girls, while I build my case for why every invitation issued in your name is not one to which you must reply *yes*.

Exhibit A: Did you know that "invitation" comes from the Latin *invitare*, which means "to invite, treat, entertain"? On the face of it, that's a nice thing...if you want to be invited, treated, and entertained and are able to accept. **But just as it's a host's prerogative to make the offer, it's yours to pass it up.**

Exhibit B: Let's say someone "invites" you to their wedding, their kid's preschool graduation, or their bimonthly drum circle in the park and they make it clear that they expect you to say nothing other than *Yes, yes, a million times yes!* This inviter is behaving like a king or queen who demands a special showing of a play because *they* want to see it under circumstances that are enjoyable and convenient for *them* — not necessarily for the twenty-two performers of *A Midsummer Night's Dream* who thought they had a midsummer night off this week. **That is not an invitation; that is a command performance.**

Exhibit C: **FUCK. THAT. SHIT.**

I understand why you might think saying no to invitations is difficult. I'm telling you it doesn't have to be. From black-tie galas to casual meet-ups, or invitations to go on a date, join a club, a committee, or a softball league, each scenario may be different, but the mechanics of RSVP'ing remain the same: **if you can't, shouldn't, or don't want to go — you can just say no.**

I've given you the tools to identify feelings of guilt and obligation and preclude them from flourishing. **Now all you need are the words** — words with which to decline, and with which to explain your decline further if you think that's necessary. Which I don't.

But Matt, if you're still reading, *MOAR TACTICS AWAIT!*

First: a note on FOMO

A big part of *Fuck No!* is **learning to say no with confidence**: in your delivery, aimed at other people; but also in who you are, what you want, and what it takes to achieve it.* This skill will serve you especially well in the face of FOMO, which those paying close attention to the INVITATIONS chapter are likely to experience more than most.

- **FOMO'ers can be introverts who don't feel like it's okay to be introverts.** Like there's something wrong with them, and they SHOULD say yes because "normal people" would WANT to say yes. If you'll excuse my language, that's bullshit. There is nothing wrong with you, and don't let arbitrary cultural norms convince you otherwise. **You need to develop confidence in WHO YOU ARE.**

- **FOMO'ers may also know what they want, but haven't come to terms with what they have to *give up* in order to get it.** And, I'm sorry guys, but this is life. You have to make decisions and live with them, or you're going to spend your days and nights so crippled by regret that you won't even enjoy the thing you chose to do instead of saying yes to the other thing. If in the end you feel you made the

---

* Come to think of it, combatting FOMO is a one-two-three punch of NFGGs: *Calm the Fuck Down,* a paean to logic and reason; *You Do You,* a handbook for self-acceptance; and the old reliable *The Life-Changing Magic of Not Giving a Fuck,* in which I beg of you to stop caring so much about other people's opinions. You've got to admit I am consistent.

wrong choice, learn from it and apply that lesson down the road. **You need to develop confidence in WHAT YOU WANT.**

In the sense of "missing out" on fun stuff, FOMO takes two forms: **Before and After.**

- **BEFORE: anxiety and indecision, fueled by potential regret.** You're weighing your options — what you WANT to do (say no) and what you're worried you SHOULD DO (say yes so you don't miss out on fun, bonding with friends, or the kind of unexpected weird and wonderful moments that future dinner party stories are built on, and which you'll then *also* be left out of). In this internal tug of war, there are no winners.

- **AFTER: anxiety, fueled by second-guessing the decision you ultimately made.** You're sitting at home (or wherever you chose to be instead), and you're worried you made the wrong call. That feeling makes it harder for you to make decisions in the future. Oh look, now we're back to BEFORE.

The struggle is real, and the cycle is vicious. It's also purely emotional, and you can counteract it with two of my favorite things: **LOGIC and REASON.** Ask yourself these questions when FOMO is afoot:

- **BEFORE**

    What are the consequences of saying no? You *definitely* get to do what you want.

What are the consequences of saying yes? You *might* have fun, but you also might be just as miserable as you expect, which is why you want to say no in the first place.

Which of those odds looks better to you? There, now place your bets with confidence.

- AFTER

Did you have the time, energy, and/or money to spend on this invitation? Possibly not.

If you did, did you want to spend it? Clearly not.

Are you happy with what you *did* choose to spend it on? If so, revel in your decision-making skills! If not, you can always choose differently next time.

If it helps, know that I have every confidence in you to get it right. (Eventually.)

No-Tip: Get out of your own head. Asking and answering all of these questions *out loud* may help you see things more clearly, or even make you realize that you're being kind of silly. Especially if you ask them out loud in a Scottish accent, which I think we can all agree is fucking delightful.

RSVP no regrets

The last invitation I said no to was a birthday dinner for a good friend.

Why?

Because my husband and I were going to have out-of-town guests arriving that same day, and although my friend said they were welcome to join, they would be fresh off eighteen hours of travel and wouldn't know anyone else at the table. And I didn't want to participate in a big group dinner that night making introductions and small talk when I could be relaxing in my own home with a couple of old amigos I only get to see about once every two years. Do you think that was rude? Or selfish?

Maybe. You said she's one of your "good" friends, but you just totally bailed on her birthday dinner even though it sounds like you could have worked it out.

Okay. Now what if I told you that we had a different plan in place to do a celebratory boat trip a couple days afterward, and that I'd already given her a nice gift? In other words, that I'm not a monster who blows off my friends on their special day, and I would be honoring her in plenty of other ways.

Oh, so there were extenuating circumstances. I guess that's fine then.

Yes, it was fine. But that's beside the point.

The thing is: I don't need anyone else to make that judgment for me, and you don't either. **It is "fine" to say no to an invitation for any reason whatsoever,** and we certainly shouldn't have to justify our decisions to the peanut gallery unless we happen to be writing an advice manual constructed for the express purpose of making this argument.

Ours is not to reason why

We covered honesty in regard to politeness, i.e., when being too much of one would render you too little of the other. **But there are benefits to being honest-yet-*nonspecific* even when politeness isn't a factor.**

You'll notice that many of my sample responses throughout the book don't require **giving a specific reason** beyond "I can't," "I shouldn't," or "I don't want to." Instead, they merely **communicate the decision you came to** as a result of those reasons (e.g., "I won't be there"), perhaps with some added flair ("But I'll be thinking of you from afar!").

That's partly because I want the advice in *Fuck No!* to be broadly applicable, and I don't know your life. But it's also because **you don't have to justify yourself to other people** as thoroughly as you may think you do.

If it makes your case handily, by all means share your specific reason for declining. ("I can't go to the party because I'll be at my grandmother's funeral.")

Later in the book, I advocate for **extra candor when it would help you avoid a similar situation** down the line. ("I can't go to the party because I have crippling social anxiety, so instead of coming up with a new lie every time you invite me somewhere, I'm just going to be straight with you now.")

And **if you have an honest-to-God scheduling conflict** (apart from a funeral, which is always a gimme) and it makes you feel better to explain the details in your decline, go right ahead.

But you don't *have to.*

In fact, sometimes giving a reason for turning down an invitation (You: "I can't go to the party because I have to get up early tomorrow.") will merely *invite* argument (Your friend Krishnan: "Who needs sleep when you've got a D.J. and an open bar?")

If you don't give a reason, you also don't have to defend it.

Nobody has time for that shit.

Getting that post-no glow

So, back to my recent birthday dinner RSVP. I told my friend "We're not going to be able to make this one," she pushed a teeny bit (as most people do), but I held firm and she accepted my answer and that was that.

Wait, wait — back up a hot second. How *did you hold firm? Like, literally,* HOW???

Whoa there, tiger! As mentioned, I am in the midst of concocting a book-length course in this very subject. But I take your point — **standing your ground *after* you say no** is just as important and valuable a lesson as working up the guts *to* say no.

Here are a few quick 'n' dirty tips to get you started:

FOR EVERY ACTION THERE IS A REACTION

Just because someone expresses their disappointment doesn't mean they're upset with you or trying to change your mind. It's fine for you to say no; it's fine for them to react to it—and if they say, "That's too bad" or "I wish you could be there," take those statements at face value. You can say "I know" or "Thanks, me too" and defuse the drama that's building inside your (and only your) head.

IT'S ONLY NATURAL

People may also respond by actively pushing for a different answer, as with "Bummer. Are you *positive* you can't make it?" or "Maybe you could just pop in for a little while?" This is standard stuff. We all want what we want and if there remains a chance we can still get it, many of us don't see the harm in pushing. (Far fewer, I hope, once they've read this book, but let's not get ahead of ourselves.) Don't get defensive; all that does is send a signal that there's an argument to be had. Which there isn't! Reiterate your position—aka what YOU want—with an "I really can't, I'm sorry" or "Unfortunately that's not going to be possible." You may be surprised how quickly this conversation will run its course.

STRAIGHT GUILT TRIPPIN'

If your adversary is laying it on thick—with a "You're seriously not coming?" or "Gosh, I never thought you'd say *no*"—but is still speaking to as opposed to yelling at you, this falls in that passive-aggressive territory we discussed on page 51. And what do we do? We IGNORE. Or we take a deep breath and ACKNOWLEDGE. We say something like "Yeah, I'm seriously not" or "Life is a journey!" You can be earnest and be honest and still keep it light. And most people don't actually want to be assholes—when they see you're not taking the bait, chances are they'll stand down, accept your answer, and just talk about you behind your back like God intended.

WE DON'T NEGOTIATE WITH TERRORISTS

Finally, if you've said no to an invitation and the inviter is beyond upset, pissed off, and/or threatening to cut ties with you completely if you don't change your mind, your other plans, or the fact that you live four states and a four hundred-dollar plane ticket away, please refer once more to page 52: "Some people just won't quit." You know what to do.

And let's not forget that **it takes two to dance this tangled tango.** I give my birthday buddy a ton of credit for dropping the issue as quickly she did. We should all be so lucky to have — and *be* — friends like her. **At the end of the day, it's much better to be someone who can take no for an answer than someone who can't, and then gives people shit about it.** (Note that for such a someone, this book makes an excellent birthday gift.)

So how can YOU get optimal results the next time someone invites you to something you can't, shouldn't, or don't want to go to?

I'm so glad you asked.

Scenari-nos: parties

● **Dinner***

Regardless of whether the day or time is convenient, group meals can be taxing for introverts, difficult for dieters, and go on too long for those who prefer to get to bed in time for that little cutie Trevor Noah to tell them what's going on in the world. Personally, I enjoy dinner parties, but I don't always want to go to every dinner party to which I am invited. If you don't either, then stop being such a people-pleaser, get over your FOMO, and say no, yo.

> "You're too kind, but my week is already packed and I need a night off from seeing people and wearing pants."

> "Thanks so much, but I'll have to let someone else drool over your eggplant parmigiana this time. *Buon appetito!*"

No-Tip: Add a compliment condiment. Like a Chipotle burrito bowl, every no can be customized. I like to lace mine with the hot sauce of high praise.

---

* Also applies to meal-based parties that occur earlier in the day. Fuck brunch, is what I'm saying.

- **Costume** (theme parties, murder mystery parties, etc.)

They're not just for Halloween and Purim anymore. If you're in the mood to put even more effort into a party than usual, go nuts. If not, go no:

> "No thanks. I haven't worn a costume since an ill-fated toga party freshman year, and for good reason."

> "Unfortunately, masks aggravate my eczema."

> *For group costume participation:*
> "Thanks for thinking of me, but I'm afraid if I manage to squeeze myself into that Village People leather daddy cop outfit, I might never be able to get out of it."

- **Viewing** (Oscars, Tonys, Super Bowls, *Bachelorette* finales, etc.)

Who doesn't love to group-watch one to four hours' worth of television that you may or may not be able to hear over all the crosstalk, and with or without adequate seating? Oh, wait: I don't. Here's how I would say an honest and polite Hard No if someone requested the pleasure of my company at a viewing party for, say, *Hamilton Live!* on Fox:

> "Thanks for the invite, but as Lin-Manuel himself might rap, I'm gonna have to 'say no to this.'"

No-Tip: Wordplay is your friend. Take it from someone who's managed to churn out five books in four years—there's a song lyric, movie title, or pithy pun to get you through any creative block, including the composition of a no. Can't make it to Walter's Army-Navy game shindig? "Sorry man, but like [one of the teams' quarterbacks], I will be passing that day."

● **Opening night (galleries, restaurants, theater, etc.)**

To show what a sport I am, I'm going to formally include book publication parties in this entry—and really, any "launch party" (except baby showers, a form of launch party that gets its own write-up in a bit). And as a periodic reminder: I'm not saying you SHOULD say no to these things. Just that if you MUST or WANT TO say no, repeat after me:

> "I'm so happy for you. Have a fabulous time and I'll be thinking of you even though I'm not able to be there."

> "Congratulations on [the event]! I'll be sure to raise a glass in your honor from afar."

● **Birthday**

Birthdays are a terrific excuse to par-tay. But if you can't make it, you can't make it. Your friend/loved one/boss/colleague/roommate/teammate/etc. isn't going to spontaneously combust if you don't put in an appearance, be it in the back room of a local dive bar or the VIP section of the MGM Grand in Las Vegas. (I've said no to both of those in recent memory and my friendships are still very much intact.) So if it's a no to this one, dawg, just RSVP accordingly and get on with your life while they celebrate theirs.

For someone you know and love:

"So sorry I can't make it, but love you!"

For someone you barely know or merely tolerate:

"Sounds like a great time, but my party hat and I are otherwise engaged. Enjoy!"

For a toddler:

"I've got plans already, but tell Skylar I said have fun in the bouncy house! Or whatever words she understands these days. I'm rusty on the language development of a two-year-old."

For a dog:

"Hey, thanks for the invite, but my humpin' leg is spoken for that weekend."

No-Tip: Do unto others. When marshalling the courage to say no, ponder how you would want someone else to respond to *your* invitation, if they couldn't or didn't want to join you. You wouldn't want them to feel pressured to say yes, would you? Correct.

● **Coming-of-age**

Be they milestones like making it to sweet sixteen or to the half-century mark, or cultural or religious ceremonies like quinceañeras and bar/bat mitzvahs, there are some birthday celebrations that carry the weight of a little or a lot more obligation. Or should I say a "sense of obligation." If you can't, shouldn't, or don't want to attend, just carry out your decision as politely as possible — recognizing both the significance of the event in the eyes of its honoree *and* your right to live your life as you please.

> "I can't believe you're about to turn [age]. Amazing! I'm sorry I won't be there to celebrate with you in person, but I hope the party is one for the record books."

> "Huge congratulations on your [milestone]. I'm sorry I'm not able to attend, but I'm so proud of you and excited to see what the next [milestone years] will bring."

- **Going-away**

If thrown by/for someone you want to say a crowded public goodbye to, great. Perhaps there will be free food: also great. But if you can't make it — again, FOR WHATEVER REASON — that's okay too. Pushovers, People-Pleasers, and Overachievers, this is your jam:

> "Ah, I'm not free that evening, but best of luck in your next big adventure!"

> "Sorry to miss this — may the corporate AmEx get one last strenuous workout."

OPTIONAL NO-AND-SWITCH:
"I can't make the party, but do you have any time for a one-on-one lunch or drink before you go?"

- **Baby showers**

Even if you love babies and the people who made them, you may not want or be able to attend every time one of your friends and family gathers in gestation celebration. Perhaps the fun is being had outside city limits and it's too far to travel for an afternoon. Maybe you have other plans that weekend. Or maybe you have a cold and you sure would hate to get anyone sick in their third trimester, so you think it's best to RSVP no and send a gift that you promise you did not touch, lick, or breathe on. In any case, you've got options:

> "I hope you have a terrific day and get all the love, attention, and EZ-Kleen spit-up cloths you can reasonably store in your apartment. You're gonna need 'em!"

> "I can't be there for the shower, but I'm sending hugs to you and the bean-to-be. And a white noise machine for your guest bedroom. Can't wait to visit!"

- **Anniversary**

Your parents' fiftieth? A probable yes for lots of reasons. Your friend's one-year-sober Taco Fest? Strong maybe. (You like to be supportive. And tacos.) But there are other commemorative fiestas that may not ring your bell, or may be held at inopportune times or inaccessible places. Depending on the circumstances, I'd go Hard No or No-and-Switch:

> "My dance card is full that night, but what a nice reason to throw a party. Have fun!"

> "I can't make it, but would love to see you sometime soon to celebrate."

- **Retirement**

Some of these require no more effort than getting up from your desk and shuffling down to conference room B at 4 p.m. to raise a glass of warm Prosecco to Lorna's forty-plus years of service. Others are nighttime affairs with an emcee, a D.J., and an inordinate amount of Midori sours and line dancing. Either way, if you have to say no, just do it in a timely (aka polite) fashion so the honoree and/or organizer isn't left in the lurch. For example:

> "What a run you've had! Congratulations, and I'll be sorry to miss the chance to make an embarrassing toast in your honor."

> "I have to pass on the party, but remember that time we [insert shared workplace memory]? Good stuff. Happy golfing!"

"Thanks for including me in [honoree's] party, but I can't make it. Hope everything goes smoothly."

Alas!

Often in the case of declining an invitation from a friend or loved one, you'd like to soften the no with some hint of "I wish I could be there," but you also want to avoid saying *precisely* that in case it would give Maggie the wrong idea about changing the date of her pottery expo to suit your schedule. If you'd like to be kind but don't want to leave the door open, "alas" is a great way to close it softly but firmly. *Alas, I won't be able to make it! Alas, I'm otherwise engaged that weekend! Alas, I'll have to catch you next time around!*

● **Weddings**

I wrote at length about weddings and related events (bachelor/bachelorette parties, bridal showers, post-wedding brunches, etc.) in *The Life-Changing Magic of Not Giving a Fuck*. Twelve whole pages — WITH DIAGRAMS. What more is there to say, especially when all you typically need to do is check the "no" box on the conveniently included RSVP card and put it in the mail?

That is how you say no to a wedding, folks. It's very simple.

But perhaps you're anxious because you just *know* you're going to have to **further explain your no** — be it to the bride or groom or to their families or to friends who wish you would have said yes so you could all split the cost of a rental car to New Haven. I hear ya. And although I maintain that you don't have to give reasons if you don't feel like it or if they don't serve you, I acknowledge that people get so fucking riled up when it comes to weddings that it doesn't hurt to go on the offensive here.

So to round out this section (and without repeating all the advice I have already dispersed in re: weddings), I'm going to share with you the reasons I gave for saying no to the weddings I haven't been able to make it to over the years, tested and approved:

For an out-of-town wedding that was held during a year that we were invited to eleven other weddings:

"We're so sorry, but we're already committed to a ton of weddings this year and we just can't get any more time off."

For an opposite-coast wedding that was held during Twelve Weddings Year and that would be preceded by a destination bachelorette party in Mexico:

"We love you guys. We are so excited that you're getting married. But we have too many weddings and not enough money and vacation days this year. We can either come on the Mexico trip *or* make it to the wedding, but we can't do both. Which would you prefer?" (They picked Mexico. *Olé!*)

For the California wedding that was held on the same weekend as another wedding we'd already said yes to and bought plane tickets for:

"Alas! We already have a wedding in Michigan that weekend."*

For the wedding of my former assistant that I *did* technically say I would be able to make it to (verbal commitment, pre-invitations) but had to renege on soon after because an extremely close friend planned her wedding for the same weekend:

"I am so, so sorry to do this, but these are some of my closest friends in the world having a small wedding full of all my other closest friends in the world. You know I adore you, but we'll know hardly anyone at your wedding and since you haven't sent out the invitations yet at least you can add two more people you love to the guest list. Instead we would be honored to take you and [her betrothed] out to an ultra-fancy dinner to celebrate and spend a few hours of quality time with you that we wouldn't get at your reception anyway. I hope you understand and that we can plan our fabulous night out very soon."

(She did and we did.)

---

* Note the use of "Alas!"

For a wedding of an old acquaintance that I didn't really understand why I was invited to since we hadn't communicated in years:

I checked "No" on the RSVP card and sent a gift. Nobody ever asked me for a reason. AND THEY WON'T ASK YOU, EITHER.

There's no need to lie or fake temporary hearing loss when someone asks you why you can't come to a wedding. **Just be honest and polite** — and if you want to lay a pair of wood-and-marble salad tongs on the happy couple, Crate & Barrel can provide. (But don't feel *obligated*; see box.)

That's a wrap!

Even if you have to roll out the no carpet on certain occasions, there are other ways to show you care. Because I'm at a point in my life where I have more disposable income than disposable time and energy, I like to send a present in lieu of my presence. But if the reason you're not going to the wedding (or the birthday cruise, or the retirement party weekend at the Kentucky Derby, etc.) is because you can't afford it, then it's possible you can't really afford to send a gift either. That's okay: don't let capitalist culture put you into credit card debt. Instead, perhaps you could record a short cell phone video wishing the honoree/s glad tidings, bring some homemade cupcakes in to work the following Monday, or make a symbolic $1 bet on your friend's horse of choice, the proceeds going to purchase them as many mint juleps as the winnings will buy. Cheers!

Gatherings

Some invitations for group events may not be RSVP-*required* parties, but you should still respond. It's rude to just not show up without letting the inviter know you don't plan to come, and there are better ways to cultivate an air of mystery than by being a jerk. Consult the following grid for **a few easy replies that can work across the board.**

	THANKS FOR THE INVITE! SORRY I CAN'T MAKE IT!	I'M NOT ABLE TO BE THERE, BUT I COULD PARTICIPATE ANOTHER WAY.	THANKS, BUT [CROWDS/ MAGIC MUSHROOMS/ BEING LOCKED IN A GLORIFIED STORAGE UNIT] ISN'T REALLY MY THING.
PROTEST	X	X	X
SPORTING EVENT	X		X
VIGIL	X	X	X
SHAMANIC RITUAL	X		X
RAVE	X		X
ESCAPE ROOM	X		X

Now you try. The next time you get invited to a casual gathering, fill in the blank chart I've provided and tell me you don't have one to three relevant replies ready and waiting. X marks the spot!

THANKS FOR THE INVITE! SORRY I CAN'T MAKE IT!	I'M NOT ABLE TO BE THERE, BUT I COULD PARTICIPATE ANOTHER WAY.	THANKS, BUT [CROWDS/ MAGIC MUSHROOMS/ BEING LOCKED IN A GLORIFIED STORAGE UNIT] ISN'T REALLY MY THING.

Pants on fire

As we shore up your fledgling naysaying practice, I want to give you a little refresher on the whole "honesty and politeness" thing. Because **when you're trying to get out of an invite *and* spare someone's feelings, you might have the urge to make up an excuse** that the inviter couldn't possibly view as a slight. Emergency appendectomy, for example. Or being relocated into Witness Protection.

And although in my earlier tutorial I allowed for fibbing that helps a *no* land more politely, you also have to commit to not being

**Nonspecific reasons
you can't make it**

Previous engagement
Other plans
Some stuff going on
"A thing"

dumb about it later. The bigger the lie, the harder that becomes — **and if you get caught, you will hurt those feelings anyway.**

For example, if you tell Nico you can't go to his birthday party because you have to "pull an all-nighter at the office" and then he sees you doing a Facebook Live from Dodger Stadium, not only are you busted, but all you've given Nico for his birthday is a complex.

Even if you're not on social media, engaging in RSVP-based wool-pulling means that **in addition to your regular calendar, you *also* have to keep a mental calendar of all the shit you said no to and why, lest you slip up.** If you're not careful, one of these days you're going to forget you told Keisha you couldn't make her Mary Kay pyramid schem — er, party — because you had a doctor's appointment at the same time. And when you completely forget about that lie on the day of the party and ask Keisha what she's up to, it's gonna take a lot of EndlessPerformance® Crème-to-Powder Foundation to cover your ass.

This is another point in favor of not giving a reason at all, but if you feel you *must* in order to avoid hurting someone's feelings, at least **keep it nonspecific.** That way, no matter what the real reason is that you're saying no, it's also the only one you have to keep track of.

It's not you, it's me

What if you're tempted to lie about why you can't, shouldn't, or don't want to accept an invitation, **not to spare someone else's feelings, but to protect your own?**

Maybe you're embarrassed to admit that the reason you can't join your friends on a weekend getaway is because you can't afford it — or you're ashamed that you *shouldn't* join them because they're headed to Atlantic City and you have a bit of a gambling problem. Maybe you're trying to lower your cholesterol and you don't want to belly up to a casino buffet full of deep-fried temptation, but you'd rather not draw attention to your true reasons for passing.

I totally understand. I'm not saying you *ought* to feel weird or embarrassed or ashamed of any of that, but I get it, and I'll just encourage you to consider this:

In cases like these, **if you're honest with the people in your life who invite you to things *now,* you're setting a damn fine precedent that may also make your life easier and less awkward *later.* You** could say something like:

> "Please don't stop inviting me to stuff, but just so you know, money is a little tight right now so I'm going to pass on this one."

> Or "Man, I'd love to be there, but me and the roulette wheel don't get along so well, if you know what I mean."

If you practice saying no with extra honesty (and politeness), others can practice hearing and responding to it the same way.

Revealing your trigger points offers your friends and family the chance to be more sensitive down the line, and to issue their invitations with thoughtful qualifications. Such as:

> "I know you haven't always wanted to do X, but if you want to come, I'd love to have you."

> Or "We want you to know you're invited, but we also want you to know we understand if you can't make it."

And being candid helps release you from after-the-fact anxiety associated with saying no. You don't have to worry if people are wondering what the "real" reason is that you're not joining the festivities, because YOU ALREADY TOLD THEM.

Isn't that a novel concept?

In the end, if you want to lie and lie hard, that's your business. And if telling an extra-tall tale turns out to be the easiest, nicest, and/or most effective way for you to say no to something, I'm not going to blow up your spot.

But I'm also not going to cover for you. Dude, Keisha is *pissed*.

Scenari-nos: dates

I'll be going into detail on romantic partners in a later chapter and, rest assured, plenty of that advice will apply to anyone you may be dating casually. But before you even get to "dating casually," you'd have to say yes to being invited on *a* date.

And maybe you're not interested.

With the caveat that I have been out of the pool since 1999, I still found it odd that so many people who responded to my survey said they had agreed to go on a date *solely* because they didn't want to hurt the other person's feelings, and then regretted it because it was exactly the incompatible waste of time they'd thought it would be.

Okaaaay...so what happens when you get asked on a second date? Or a third?

Assuming your initial aversion holds, how much more time and expensive hair product are you going to waste on this self-inflicted guilt trip when **you could be honest and polite,** say something like "I don't want to hurt your feelings, but I just don't think we're a match," and leave it at that? For example:

If it's an invitation from a known entity — be it a friend, a coworker, or the person who sits across from you on the bus every morning — and you want to be chill about it:

"To be honest, that's not something I'm interested in pursuing, but I appreciate you asking and hope we can still be [friends/colleagues/easygoing fellow commuters]."

If you don't want to be chill about it:

"Yeah...no. I'm not gonna lie — this is weird and I'm not sure we can keep being [friends/coworkers/easygoing fellow commuters]."

If it's a setup that you're not down for:

"I've seen the pics and listened to your pitch, and I do not think this person is, as you say, 'perfect for me.' For someone? No doubt! But not I."

If it's an attempted meet-cute, and you want to be nice:

"I'm really flattered you [came over to talk to me/bought me a drink/etc.], but I don't think this is in the cards. Have a great evening."

If you want to GTFO:

"Not gonna happen."

If it's a blind date and you've seen the light and it says Stop:

"I'm assuming you feel the same way I do and this won't be going any further, but I wish you all the best." (Honest yet still sneakily polite, this **Proactive No** allows the other person to save face by agreeing even if they *didn't* feel the same way you do. Classy.)

I know when that hotline bling, that can only mean one thing

Are you tired of being someone's booty call? If so, try texting back a different .GIF every time until they get the message. The Grumpy Cat "NOPE" and the Leonardo-DiCaprio-in-*Wolf-of-Wall-Street* "Absolutely fucking not" are both strong options. You could also Power No it: no answer, no reply, no last-minute bikini wax. Better yet, mute this siren song altogether by blocking their number. And hey, if what you want is for your gentleperson caller to ask you on a real date instead of a last-minute tryst, perhaps absence will motivate the heart to buy you dinner and a movie next time? Or you could also just ask them out yourself, you modern human, you.

Matchmaker, Matchmaker, make me a match!

In terms of brokering romance — if being asked to *facilitate* dates (or, um, other stuff) between people you know makes you uncomfortable, there's a Hard No for that too:

"OOH, CAN YOU HOOK ME UP WITH…"

…your friend?	"If I do that and it works out, I'm going to find out a lot more about your penis than either of us ever wanted me to know."
…your roommate?	"You have lovely hair, but I don't want to wake up to it my shower drain."
…your sister?	"I'd prefer to be the only one of us who's ever shared a bed with her, so no."
…your boss?	"She likes self-starters."
…your ex?	"No, although given that you even think it's okay to ask me that, I imagine you two would get along well."
…your dad?	"Categorically not."

Scenari-nos: joining up and in

Taking it back to Book Club Janet and her Chapters & Chardonnay shenanigans, I want to close the loop on invitations with ones **to *join* stuff—be it a club, team, or committee.**

Maybe you don't have time, or can't afford the membership fees. Maybe you're the kind of person who prefers to walk the streets playing Pokémon Go rather than joining a soccer league or an intramural water polo team. That's cool; there's nothing wrong with being a lone Pikachu.

Personally, I tend to avoid team play because I'm a little *too* competitive and I don't like having to depend on others in my quest for victory. It's better if I just say, "No thanks, you guys have fun without me at Trivia Night." Because if I show up and know that *All in the Family* is the answer to "Which television series used the toilet-flush sound for the first time?" but the other bozos on my team overrule me and go with *M.A.S.H.*—and we lose—then all I get to say is "I told you so." And that's never as satisfying as I want it to be.

Anyway, whatever the reason you're disinclined to join, you can treat such an invitation just like you would one to a party or gathering. Be honest and polite. Throw in a **"Thanks for thinking of me"** or an **"I wish I could."**

And you can always lean heavily on **"I don't have time,"** since it's common knowledge that round-robin tournaments and planning committees suck the hours out of a calendar faster than I can finish a coco loco at the beach on Sunday afternoon. (Which, for the record, is pretty fucking fast.) A few examples:

"Any interest in playing for the company softball team? We could really use a shortstop."

"Trust me, you're better off with someone else in the hole. Go get 'em, Initech Tigers!"

"Would you be interested in co-chairing the crafts committee?"

"Not really. I actually enrolled the kids at camp to *free up* some time for me this summer."

"The Corgi Appreciation Society would be pawsitively honored to have you as a member."

"Thanks for thinking of me! I do love a small dog, but I prefer to appreciate them on my own, for maximum effect."

Finally, this one goes out to the Pushovers. I know you're out there, and it's just your luck to get called up on stage.

- **Audience participation**

If you volunteered for something and then regretted having to handwrite three hundred place cards for that charity dinner or blow up a bouquet of penis balloons for your friend's bachelorette party, it sucks to be you, but you still chose to do it of your own free will. However, if you were hounded into "volunteering" by a magician or a stand-up comedian or a Blue Man and now you're getting chopped in two, heckled, and covered Jell-O, it wasn't a fair fight. In the future, ways to avoid guinea-pigging under duress include:

"No, I don't want to do that."

<vigorous head shake>

<point at the guy next to you>

Shout "Not it!" and touch your finger to your nose in the universal signal that you have taken yourself out of the running.

Cut a bitch.

Shit, something came up!

We're nearly finished with the first dedicated chapter on ways to say *cha*,* so naturally it's time to throw you a curveball.

What if you *already accepted* an invitation, but now you want to rescind your commitment? (Perhaps because you've been reading a

---

* That's Zulu for "no."

certain illuminating tome that has shown you the error of your yessy ways…) Interesting. Let me ask you this:

Would changing your mind mean you'd be leaving someone in the mega-lurch—such as deciding you really don't feel like being a bridesmaid in your friend's wedding when she's already processing down the aisle to the dulcet tones of Céline Dion?

Or is this a simple matter of begging off a casual day at the ballpark (and eating the cost of your bleacher seat instead of two hot dogs and a box of Cracker Jacks)?

Oh, and are you a consistently annoying flake? Or is this a onetime deal?

If you answer these questions honestly and decide that **the consequences of switching sides are manageable and minimal** compared to those of gritting your teeth and bearing three hours of your niece's fourth grade chorus concert, then I say it's well within your rights to issue an updated response.

Plans evolve. "Previous commitments" get "remembered." These things happen.

Muster your best *Alas!*, strap on an *I'm sorry,* and issue an update. There may be a little discomfort (especially for first-timers), but you'll be relieved when you're home with a glass of Pinot and a bowl of Cheez-Its, catching up on *Shrill* on Hulu instead of listening to a prepubescent rendition of "Let There Be Peace on Earth."

Also shrill, much less enjoyable.

FuckNotes: Invitations Edition

And now, to close our chapter on invitations and appropriate responses thereto, I present the first installment of . . . FuckNotes!

(Remember when I told you this book would contain fill-in-the-blank exercises akin to Mad Libs™ that would not be called Mad Libs™ because the Mad Libs™ name belongs to someone else? These are those.)

FuckNotes are templates that help you craft a no best suited to your individual situation. You'll find three at the end of each chapter, and until I get my act together to come out with a whole line of FuckNotes activity books, feel free to Xerox them and staple the copies together to form a go-to cheat sheet for all those times that you can't, shouldn't, or just don't want to.

For invitations, gather the following:

- The event you've been invited to
- A conflicting event, if any (optional)
- A bad feeling you do *not* wish on the inviter
- An expression of support for the inviter (e.g., "love you," "am proud of you")

- Personal issues that preclude your attendance, if any (optional)

- A positive adjective

Then, mix 'n' match to form your no. It's that easy! And you can always embellish after the fact if you think it's necessary, although you know how I feel about that, Matt.

If you CAN'T

Alas, I can't come to your _____
                                          event you're invited to

[because I have a(n) _____]. I hope
                              conflict, if any

you won't be _____, you know I
                        bad feeling

_____. Have a(n) _____ time!
expression of support/   positive adjective
     love/etc.

If you SHOULDN'T

Unfortunately, I won't be able to make it to

your _____. [_____ makes it
        event you're invited to   personal issue, if any

difficult for me to do this kind of thing.] Have

a(n) _____ time!
            positive adjective

If you JUST DON'T WANT TO

Hey, sorry I can't make it to your _____,

event you're invited to

but I appreciate the invite and I hope you have

a(n) _____ time!

positive adjective

FAVORS

free advice, small loans, and big asks of all varieties

I want you to know that if you have the time, energy, money, and desire to do someone a favor, that is really kind of you and you should be commended for it. You're the best! But I also want you to know that **declining to do a favor** — for someone you love or live with or for a stranger in the hotel lobby — **doesn't automatically make you an unkind person.** In fact, I hope that if you are an unkind person you are not reading my book, because I don't want your money. Unkind people can suck it.

I simply doubt very much that you can say yes all the time. Nor should you be expected to. So in this chapter, I'll walk you through no's to easy errands and extensive physical labor; to quick cash infusions and big-time bailouts; and to requests for professional or ew-that's-way-too-personal advice.

We'll look at favor requests that you have time to ponder and real-time asks that require swift and decisive action; ones for which the requester offers nothing in return (either because they have nothing to offer, because they are oblivious, or because they are kind of a dick); and also ones the asker hopes to someday repay (such as monetary loans or investments), but to which you are still entitled to say no if the terms do not appeal to you.

Last but not least, I'll speak to **favors you may be *offered* and which you do not wish to accept.** Because not everybody wants another piece of pie, Gretchen, no matter how famous the old family recipe. (Unless it's chocolate cream, in which case I would gladly accept the favor of you constructing a conveyor belt that runs directly between the refrigerator and my yawning gullet. Thanks!)

Hey, can you do something for me?

Favors people might ask that this book will help you say no to

Putting together IKEA furniture

Carpooling

Schlepping heavy equipment they "forgot"

Getting a ride to/from the airport

Peeing in a cup to cheat a drug test

Bringing your grill over because they don't have one

Doing all the grilling because they don't know how

Holding their stuff because they won't suck it up and get a man purse

From "Can you feed my dog for six weeks while I go on a hot yoga retreat with my new lover" to "Can you finish this Power-Point for tomorrow's meeting? I got tickets to the Raiders game — thanks!" there are millions of favors someone might ask you to do for them and only so many hours in the day or so much heavy-lifting your old bones can take.

Once-in-a-while help and bailouts? No problemo! But if you have friends, family, or coworkers who abuse your favor-granting prowess, take heed, for **you do not have to say yes all the time just because you've said yes a few times before.**

Instead, keep your hernia in check, your Wednesday night free, and your Kate Spade tote unsullied by your boyfriend's extra gym socks, by using one of these **easy-peasy ripostes that are suitable for most favor-based scenari-nos:**

"Alas, I'm not available."

"No can do, friend-o."

"I can't help you this time."

"Ah, sorry, got too much on my plate this week!"

"Nope."

Or how about **big, giant, involved favors that involve big, giant, involved sacrifices on your part?** Like... I don't know... helping someone make a baby?*

Sperm donation, surrogacy, and other family planning assists

If someone asks you to help create or carry their child, chances are you have a close enough relationship that this isn't *completely* out of the question, or at least the person asking hopes it might not be. Regardless, it's delicate territory, and if it gets sprung on you like Janet Jackson's nipple at the Super Bowl halftime show, you can say, **"I'm honored to be asked, but I'll need some time to think about it."** Then if you eventually decide your swimmers should stay confined to their own lanes or your pool is closed to outside business, try one of these empathetic replies on for size:

---

* All I can say is, I promised you this one back on page 6 and I am a woman of my word. I am also a woman who beats jokes into the ground over and over until they become unfunny and then funny again — or at least until I think they've become funny again.

"I love you so much and want you to be happy, but after a lot of soul-searching, I don't think I am prepared for this responsibility."

"I wish I could be the one to help you have a family, but I've given this a lot of thought and I've realized it's just not going to work for me, for a number of reasons. I would be happy to share my reasons if you like, but I understand if you just want to move on."

NOTE: Similar language works if you get asked to take legal guardianship over someone's children should anything happen to the parents. Oddly, none of my friends have ever brought up this subject with me, but like the U.S. Coast Guard motto goes: *Semper paratus!*

Hey, can you pick something up on your way?

Here's the deal: if it's really on my way and a certain someone asked before I already passed the store where it's located, and it's not something ridiculous like a cord of firewood or a tank of live eels, then sure. But if it's extremely inconvenient, heavy, dangerous, or absurd—and especially if this certain someone *always* asks me to pick up shit on my way and at the last minute—then no, sorry, can't do that. Why? Oh, I'm running late and I passed the aquarium fifteen minutes ago and my car is already full of predatory sea birds. Sorry, maybe you can ask Seth to go? See you soon!

Premature rejection

A fun and educational part of each No Fucks Given Guide is when I turn my personal shame into teachable moments. And so, I give you **The Story of the Prayers of the Faithful.**

Picture it: Ireland. The Wild Atlantic Way. Summer of 2012. My husband and I had traveled 3,000 miles to attend the wedding of a native Irishwoman and one of my favorite people in the world. Her name is Louise.

After enjoying my first Guinness on Irish soil (I hate to contribute to stereotypes, but it really is better there), we faffed about for a day or two in advance of the nuptials. One of those afternoons, Louise invited me to tag along with her on some bridal errands and we wound up at her parents' house, where I helped her trim her veil and watched some cute woodland creatures skipping across the verdant emerald lawn.

Again, Ireland, really living up to the stereotype.

It was here that she posed the question "Would you like to say a few words in church tomorrow?"

Cut to me thinking it was weird that she'd ask me if I wanted to get up during her wedding and give, like, a church toast, since she knows I'm not much for God and related oratory and rhetoric.

I should have known better and sought clarification. Instead, I responded with a hasty "Oh no, no need!"

At this point in our conversation, Louise sort of blinked and then said carefully, "Perhaps I wasn't clear. I'm asking if you would do me the *honor* of reading one of the Prayers of the Faithful during the ceremony."

Ah. Gotcha.

Thankfully, she granted me a do-over, and this time it was an enthusiastic yes to my dear friend, for whom I would do a lot of things I don't normally engage in — including speaking in church and eating that floppy ham that Irish people insist on calling "bacon." And I'm pleased to report that my husband says I didn't smirk even a little bit during my turn at the pulpit, despite the fact that my assigned prayer was the one about wishing the happy couple "the pitter patter of little feet."*

So, dear reader, this has been your friendly neighborhood anti-guru reminding you that **before you answer a favor request (or any request, really) with a negative, first be sure you understand the question.** Just in case you may a) have actually wanted to say yes, or b) wish you had handled it a tad differently.

Sláinte.

Hey, can you spot me some cash?

Giving away money is a lovely pastime. It's one of my favorite things to do, and I'm fortunate to be in a position in my life these days where I can do it with some regularity. Good times! But that doesn't mean that I always *will*. I have my reasons, and you probably do too. Maybe you can give it away but you don't want to. Or you want to, but you shouldn't. Maybe you can't or shouldn't, and you don't really *want* to explain why. Touché.

As you know by now, I don't give a loose goose what your reasons

---

* "Sorry," Louise said after I agreed to publicly urge her to breed, in the House of God no less. "I know you hate children, but I didn't want to give you the one about dead relatives and the rest were spoken for."

are. You do you. But if you're having trouble saying no to giving loans, declining to make donations, or turning down investment opportunities — put your wallet away.

I've got this round.

Donations

"Now isn't a good time for me."

This is a terrific all-purpose no, but especially for monetary asks. It's honest but polite, and also nonspecific. (*"Never* would be a good time for me" may be more honest, but it's less polite. See how that works?) It's also equally good for use on family, friends, and total strangers. Recall what we discussed in part I about alumni organizations, political campaigns, and anyone making a cold call to divest you of your cold hard cash: they definitely have another number on speed dial. It costs you nothing to let them use it.

Loans

"This isn't going to work for me."

A variation on the "It's just not possible" No-Tip from page 38, this makes

> **Other things you may not wish to lend, for which "This isn't going to work for me" is also an adequate response**
>
> Your toothbrush
> Your underwear
> Your favorite shirt
> Your signed first edition of *Harry Potter*
> Your photo ID
> Your car
> The only decent pair of scissors you've ever owned

it less about *you* not wanting or being able to loan money, and more about *the terms of the loan itself* not being feasible. Maybe it doesn't "work" for you because you don't have the dough, or because you've already said yes three times and you'd rather not get a reputation as a walking ATM. Or because although you don't want your buddy to lose his home, you also don't want to be responsible for guaranteeing his mortgage given what you know about his lust for Bitcoin. The reasons don't matter; your answer is still no.

However, what if it's not the financial layout itself that's the problem, but the idea of acting as banker to your friend or family member for five to ten years while they pay you back? In that case, you could always **counteroffer with a No-and-Switch gift:**

> "I'd like to help, but not as a loan. How about I give you [an amount of money you feel comfortable with] free and clear, and you pay it forward someday?"

Investments

"I'd rather not get financially involved on the front end, but I'll be first in line when your [invention/service/etc.] goes live. Good luck!"

Investment opportunities are similar to loans, except the payback (if any) is usually tied to performance of a concept — which your friend Grace has even less control over than amassing her startup capital. Your money will double *if* the underwater cat circus takes off. Or your shares will be worth something *if* the solar-powered sex toys company goes public someday. And if the potential return on investment isn't worth it or seems too risky, **you have every right to pass on the opportunity and contribute solely good wishes** toward your pal's future fame and fortune.

If they don't invite you to the ribbon-cutting ceremony, it's no skin off your teeth. You had a previous engagement that day anyway.

<Wink>

Hey, can I pick your brain?

Beware the brain-pickers! Like information zombies, they feed on your hard-won, painstakingly acquired knowledge and expertise, slowly draining *you* of time and energy as *they* grow more informed.

Unlike zombies, you can't always see them coming (what with the lack of rotting flesh falling in clumps from their undead faces), so it's up to you to remain vigilant — especially at cocktail parties, waiting on lines, in public restrooms at industry events,* and when logged in to Facebook Messenger, a service that FAR too many people think is appropriate for sending out-of-the blue volleys to folks they don't know or haven't spoken to in fifteen years to ask for free professional advice, services, and connections.

Sigh.

---

* I speak from experience, and from the ladies' room at the Staples Center during Book Expo America 2008.

Now, to be fair, sometimes allowing your brain to be picked is a simple matter of regurgitating a few facts or opinions you already possess. **It's easy, and you get karma points.**

Sometimes **it's not that easy, but you agree anyway** because you're nice like that.

And other times, **it's just too much to ask, and you have to say no even if it feels icky to do so.**

In any case, **once you've been asked, the ball is in your court.** You better serve it like vintage Serena and put an end to this conversation before it gets out of hand like the 2019 Australian Open quarterfinals.

Can we grab a coffee?

I've always found "coffee dates" an unappealing proposition. Partly because coffee is a thing I typically consume in great haste first thing in the morning when I'm unfit to converse with my cats, let alone other people. But also, how much meaningful conversation can you really have over a coffee? Even less, if you order espresso. Organizing a whole encounter around drinking it feels profoundly inefficient. And beyond that, requests for coffee dates are a known precursor to brain-picking. I'm sure plenty of people make such overtures with no ulterior motive, but when I hear "Can we grab a coffee?" I'm inclined to respond "No, but you can ask me a favor without the pomp and circumstance and bamboo stir sticks, and we'll take it from there."

In the next few pages, I'll provide **scripts and strategies that are high on tact and diplomacy,** and low on you getting cornered at your kid's Pee Wee hockey game explaining to Marco's dad the seven million steps necessary to form a 501(c)(3) under U.S. tax code. Just because you're an accountant doesn't mean you have to "account" for other people's unwillingness to make an appointment for a paid consultation.

BONUS: It's not just professional advice you're getting asked to provide *gratis;* **it's personal advice too!** And sometimes that's icky in a different way. Later, I'll share a few tips for avoiding or putting an end to conversations that make you go *Hmm.*

Advance no-tice

For starters, let's assume **you've been asked for free professional advice** of a lengthy, involved nature, and that you have neither the time nor desire to dole it out. Let's also assume you've been asked in writing — email is often how these things go — and you have the luxury of taking some time to compose a response. (I'll deal with real-time asks in a few. Don't get cocky.)

Here's your three-step path to an effective no:

STEP 1: SLOW YOUR NO ROLL

This isn't an invitation with an RSVP-by date. You can be polite without being particularly speedy. Conjure that too-hard talisman we discussed on page 61, or another favor request that went haywire. Do you really want to get stuck on the phone again for an hour like you did with your friend's Aunt Marigold who was hoping you could give her some pointers on securing funding for her CBD toiletries business? Especially without the aid of one of the cannabinoid bath bombs that Marigold has, shockingly, yet to mass-produce?

If the answer is no, you can afford the ten minutes it'll take to decide, and *then* type out a response that gets your point across gently but firmly.

STEP 2: MAKE IT BRIEF (AND DON'T BE AN ASSHOLE)

When you're ready to issue your polite no, don't undo all the good you're about *to* do by running on like a Hemingway sentence. Keep it short and to the point, sprinkle in a "Best of luck" or "Sorry I couldn't be of more help" and then sign off, sister. (See page 161; there's a FuckNote for that.)

And unless warranted by a request that was assholic in and of itself — such as your ex-BFF from high school popping up in your DMs twenty years later to beg a career contact without even acknowledging/apologizing for what she did on prom night '98 (seriously, the *balls* on that one) — try to be nice, or at least neutral. A bridge is a terrible thing to burn.

STEP 3: MOVE ON

Delete the original advice-asking email, stat. You don't want it haunting your inbox and convincing you you're a jerk every time you look at it. If you let it hang out, eventually it might guilt you into reconsidering, reaching out, and offering two hours of unpaid consultation as penance for your earlier lapse in decency.

Congrats! You just spent *more* time on this.

Have you considered Googling it?

I'm not trying to be bitchy—swear to Beyoncé—but Sergey Brin and Larry Page didn't amass their sinister and all-knowing information empire to make research *more* difficult for the person asking you, a high school track-and-field coach, to give them the rundown on the top ten college javelin programs for their teen son to consider when he begins his applications next year. Seriously, it just took me less than five minutes to dig up Project Javelin Gold—a clinic out of LSU staffed by multiple Olympians. (Geaux Tigers!) In many cases, Google will give more thorough and up-to-date advice than you can. As long as you point that out in a friendly fashion, it turns out you're doing someone a favor after all. Aren't you sweet.

No-tip: Cut it, paste it, and forget it. Gunning for "Mr. Nice Guy" on your gravestone? Develop a short list of resources that can be easily plunked into an email when your chiropractor's daughter is hoping to "come in for an informational interview" and you want to help but only have sixty seconds, not sixty minutes, to spare. I never did this for people who wanted to break into publishing, but I do have a doc on my laptop ready to go with recommendations on where to eat and drink in New Orleans. So I feel I'm doing my part for humanity.

Coming up next: I promised you tips on real-time requests, so let's take this out of the inbox and into the fire…

The no-ment of truth

If you met me at a party, you'd probably deem me a "people person." I smile. I joke. I set my laser beams to charm, almost always with utmost sincerity. But my crowd-working mojo lands me in the hot seat when people I barely know turn "What do you do?" chit-chat into "That's cool! Hey, can you do me a favor?" before the canapés can come around twice. It took me many years and a lot of deer-in-headlights yessing before I figured out **how to issue live, in-person no's with confidence.**

These days the no's flow easily and naturally from my lips. No more awkward pauses or frantic mental shuffling for excuses, and no caving to the easier-in-the-moment "Sure thing!" that will have me resentfully rearranging my to-do list next week when the bill comes due.

Would you like to know how I do it?

(That's not a trick question. You are permitted to say yes here.)

The answer is, I come prepared. I call this trick **No Before You Go.**

For example, if I'm going anywhere that the subject of me being a writer might come up and I suspect I might get asked to read someone or their brother's or their brother's urologist's manuscript, I pack a few go-to responses in my Nine West clutch:

"Can I send you my manuscript?"

"Alas, I barely have time to read my own pages right now."

"Can I send you my brother's manuscript?"

"Alas, I barely have time to read my own pages right now — but please send him my best regards for following his dream."

"Can I send you my brother's urologist's manuscript?"

"Alas, I barely have time to read my own pages right now — but if my schedule opens up and I need a free urinalysis, maybe we can do some business."

Whatever your area of expertise — and if you think your sister's housewarming party tonight is prime hunting ground for brain-pickers — take a moment to **prep yourself before you pledge yourself.**

If you're a doctor...
"I can't give an accurate diagnosis two martinis in, but I recommend calling your GP in the morning."

Or if the encounter is not one in which you can plead minor intoxication:

"I have a personal policy against giving medical advice outside the office. I know a guy who got sued for that, and it was even less pretty than that rash you just showed me."

If you're a lawyer...
"That's not really my field."

Or if it is your field:

"I don't think you want to know how much I bill to answer that question."

If you're a teacher...
"Things change so quickly! I wouldn't know where to begin designing a curriculum that will guarantee Maximilian entry into his top choice college in seven years."

If you're a student...
"I have no fucking idea how I got into Penn, but I'm sure if you call the Admissions Office you could talk to someone about what they're looking for."

If you're an electrician...
"I *could* tell you how to install that ceiling fan, but then it's on me if you fry yourself, and my insurance premium is already too high."

If you're a musician...
"You don't need me, dude. There is most definitely a YouTube video that can teach you how to play 'Stairway to Heaven.'"

Those examples were fun and easy to dream up, and I don't even have a dog in this fight. Surely with your breadth of real-life experience, you can do even better. Why not use the space below to jot down a few go-to one-liners?

NO BEFORE YOU GO

_____

_____

_____

_____

_____

The possibilities are endless — much like that conversation you were having with Gerald from your aunt's choir group who found out you're a dermatologist and was wondering if you'd be willing to pop into the stairwell and take a look at a mole on his back that seems like it could be serious.

And since we're on this topic: **don't be like Gerald.**

Is there a doctor in the house?

I recently experienced a bout of ringworm. It's gross and inconvenient and mildly terrifying if you don't know what you're dealing with — which I didn't, until I went to a real, live doctor who examined me and wrote me a prescription and to whom I paid real, live money for his services. (Incidentally, this is how I found out that ringworm is not actually a worm, but rather a fungus. Like athlete's foot or jock itch for your non-foot, non-crotch regions. You learn something new every day, kids!)

You may wonder where I'm going with this line of storytelling. Fair. I am known for my roundabout ways of getting to a point.

The thing is, I also happen to be personally acquainted with several medical doctors, some of whom are even close friends. But did I text, email, or DM any of them photos of my oozing wound for diagnosis and treatment protocol? Nope, sure didn't. I thought about it a few times, but then I also thought, *Friends who labored through years of medical school, residency, fellowships, and grueling twelve-hour E.R. shifts to get where they are now do not exist to be your personal WebMDs.*

So while *Fuck No!* is really a book about helping you refuse inappropriate or burdensome asks, please consider this my PSA on behalf of every professional friend or acquaintance whose brain YOU may be tempted to pick the next time you run into THEM at a barbecue.

Two-way street, and all that.

Hey, can I get your opinion on something?

Moving on from professional asks to personal ones...

These could be simple and low-impact — like your coworker Marsha wanting to run some granite samples by you to narrow down her choices for her kitchen reno, or you asking me if you should have your birthday party at the bowling alley or the tiki bar. Both excellent choices, but I vote flaming drinks.

They could be more serious or complicated — like your little sister looking for guidance in choosing a college, or your friend Anna thinking that maybe it's time for *her* little sister to quit drinking, and can she talk this out with you to help her strategize?

Relationships are built, in part, on seeking and dispensing advice and being there for each other in tough times. And on endless text chains with pics of you in the dressing room at Target trying on bathing suits that will only see the light of day if three out of four friends agree they are [fire emoji].

You may be happy to act as a sounding board. And once again, this is not a treatise against doing favors and giving advice entirely. Obviously I'm keen on advice-dispensing, or we wouldn't be having this conversation.

***Fuck No!* is simply here for the times when you can't, shouldn't, or don't want to go there.** Maybe it's awkward. Maybe you don't have time to get into it right now. Maybe you never want to get into it. For example:

> Should your friend break up with that girl he thought he was going to marry, and who keeps stomping on his heart like the glass at their prospective Jewish wedding? (Yes, but he may not actually want to hear that from you. And if they get married anyway, there's no striking your testimony from the record.)

Should your none-too-bright coworker quit before he knows whether he got in to grad school? (Probably not, but you'd rather steer clear of this guy's life decisions. He worships Ed Hardy and seemingly uses AXE body spray as mouthwash.)

What if your parents want to give polyamory a go? What do you think about that, sweetie? Any tips?

BOUNDARY ALERT! Put those sheep on lockdown and **do *yourself* a favor by saying no.** Whether you wish to avoid getting inappropriately entangled in a colleague's personal life, or you're anxious about advising a close friend or family member on something that lies outside your comfort zone, **you've got two ways to go here, champ:**

FLOAT LIKE A BUTTERFLY

Sometimes when you're faced with a clear, specific request for personal advice, the best response is a vague, unspecific answer. Like, if your roommate asks you whether she should confront your mutual friend about a Saturday night indiscretion involving someone's ex-boyfriend, you may prefer to stay out of it, and off of everybody's shit list. Possible responses to a request of this nature include:

"I don't think I'm the best person to advise you on that."

"This decision is really up to you."

"I just don't know what to tell you."

STING LIKE A BEE

Other times it's better for everyone if you deliver your Hard No with a reason in tow, such as:

> "I can't tell you what to do here, because I don't fully understand all of the factors in play."

> "I shouldn't weigh in on this, because I know we don't share the same view of the potential outcome."

> "I don't want to give you my opinion, because I'm worried it may come between us."

Remember what I said in the intro to this chapter: declining to do a favor — including getting all up in someone's business at their request — does not make you a bad person. Per the above, there are honest and polite ways to scuttle this line of inquiry altogether.

And if you *do* have the time and energy to talk, but think it's unwise to level an opinion on whether Sharon was wrong to sleep with P.J. ("Technically, you guys were on a break..."), you can **stick with empathetic expressions of support, well-wishes, and solidarity.**

---

5 non-judgy, non-committal phrases for trying times

"I'm sorry you're dealing with this."

"I feel for you."

"This is really tricky."

"Do you think it would help you to talk to a professional?"

"I'll be right back with some ice cream."

Serial no-ffenders

You might have someone in your life who asks for advice on a regular basis. You might even call it a constant basis. You might even call it "OMFG if you text me one more time asking if you should forgive Sharon and P.J. I'm going to go back in time and sterilize their mothers myself just to put an end to this shit."

At such times, call upon your H&P training.

You needn't be rude or dismissive, and you don't have to shame anyone into submission. What you can do is **encourage them to be less dependent on you and more confident in their own decision-making skills.** It's a little effort on your part at the outset, but certainly no more than you've already been expending as a freelance counselor/therapist, for which you do not get paid and which takes up too many hours per week that you could otherwise spend watching college hoops or meditating on the mysteries of the universe.

Plus, you'll be helping them more in the long run. Give a man a fish, you feed him for a day. Teach a man to solve his own fucking problems, you gain hours of uninterrupted me-time. It's an ancient Chinese proverb. Look it up.

The next time your friend (or sibling, roommate, neighbor, etc.) asks you for the fifteenth time what they should do about their delinquent employee or how they should handle their latest breakup or half-baked business idea, try one of the below responses to get them to start looking inward:

"You've asked my advice on this a few times before, and it keeps happening. Maybe it's time to trust your own instincts."

"Imagine I've gone backpacking in the Himalayas for a month with no cell service. What would you do?"

"I could give you my advice, but we've established that you never take it. So I'm going to pass on this one and save us both the time it will take you to get to 'doing whatever you want.' Sound good?"

Okay, fine, that last one was a little harsh. **Some people require tough love** — especially the ones who keep you up until all hours of the night, multiple nights a week, asking you to describe in detail the steps they should take to extricate themselves from an ongoing college hookup that will NEVER evolve into a mature, rewarding adult relationship and then they still go back to the guy whose claim to fame is making them wear a *dog collar* to prove their loyalty, and you know what?

Mazel tov. I'm out.

Bye, Felicia

I don't know how I got from refusing to pick up a tank of live eels on the way to a party to putting an end to a toxic relationship, but here we are. Entire books could be, should be, and probably are devoted to saying no to accepting negative, emotionally draining people into your life. And that may seem like an intimidating proposition, but is it more intimidating than being regularly abused or taken advantage of by those who purport to care about you? Seems unlikely. Maybe I'll write a whole book about it myself someday, because *hoo baby I have some STORIES*. But for now, you can use the tools I've already provided: valuing your resources, weighing consequences, and setting and enforcing boundaries. Whether you're pushing back against requests for payday loans or bad behavior by poisonous people, Saying "This isn't going to work for me" is always an option.

I'm going to make you an offer you *can* refuse

To conclude the FAVORS chapter on a lighter note, let's look at **yes-traps of another kind:** *offers* **of help.**

These may present as innocent attempts by someone to take some stress off of your hands, or more enervating endeavors to do shit for you that you do not wish to be done.

You know the ones I'm talking about — like "Are you sure you don't want me to look that over and give you some feedback?" Or "You need warm socks! Can I get you some socks?"*

To make this as easy as possible, I've put together a selection of

---

* Had my husband declined an offer of warm socks — which he did not need or want, but felt compelled to accept — he might never have slipped and fallen down the wooden stairs at my parents' house, necessitating shoulder surgery four months later. You live, you learn, you insist you're fine to go barefoot.

other well-intentioned tenders and ways to respond if you wish to decline with both grace and finality:

A NO FOR ALL OCCASIONS

OFFER	RESPONSE
"Would you like some more [gross food item]?"	"No thank you."
"Do you need a hand with that [heavy item you're almost finished carrying up the stairs, which would necessitate you stopping and re-balancing it just to go ten more feet with assistance]?"	"No thank you."
"I've got tickets to [mystifyingly popular jam band] if you're interested."	"No thank you."
"May we gate check your carry-on bag [that you so carefully packed in for the express purpose of not having to wait at baggage claim on the other end]?"	"No thank you."
"I'm getting a Coors Light. Want one?"	"Never."

Yes, that was a somewhat labored way of making a simple point, but given that you are reading a multi-hundred-page book about saying a two-letter word, I think it's fair play. And despite what Podcast Matt might think, **"No thank you" is a totally reasonable, honest, polite, all-around appropriate response to a whole lotta offers.**

But if it's still not enough for you, there's always FuckNotes...

FuckNotes: Favors Edition

Gather the following:

- Expression of sympathy or regret/apology (e.g., "Wish I could help" or "Sorry")
- The favor you've been asked to do
- An honest, polite reason why you can't/shouldn't do it (optional)
- Offer to help another time (optional)
- Alternate solution to get the favor done

If you CAN'T

_____, but I can't _____
expression of sympathy/apology   favor you've been asked to do

[because I _____]. Maybe you could
                    reason why you can't

try _____? [Or if you're flexible, I
          alternate solution

could help you _____.]
                    alternate timeframe

If you SHOULDN'T

_____, but I'm not able to _____
expression of sympathy/apology   favor you've been asked to do

[because I _____]. Maybe you could
                reason why you shouldn't do it

try _____ instead? Good luck!
          alternate solution

If you JUST DON'T WANT TO

_____, but that's not going to work
expression of sympathy/apology

for me. Maybe you could try _____
                                alternate solution

instead? Good luck!

PERMISSION & CONSENT

a mini-chapter, if I may

Not necessarily an invitation, nor always purely a favor, **permission is its own brand of request.**

For example, someone who asks "Can I rub your shoulders?" may technically be *inviting* you to receive a massage, but they're not looking for an RSVP so much as seeking your approval to commence kneading. And the lady who asks if you'll trade seats with her on the plane so her dog can look out the window is in some sense asking you to do her (and her dog) a favor — but that's because she knows Row 12 isn't a park bench with unassigned seating and she can't just plop herself and Woof Blitzer down wherever; **she has to ask permission, and it's up to you to give consent.**

(Then there are the craftily phrased ones like "Are you done with that?" which really means "Can I help myself to half your sandwich?" The answer to both of which is "Slow your roll there, Slim Jim. I'll pass my plate over if and when the answer is yes, and not a moment sooner." Add optional hand swat/fork stab as needed.)

In the first half of this pint-sized, specialized chapter, I'll walk you through some popular permission-begging, consent-seeking scenari-nos and show you how to demur, deflect, and decline as needed. As for the second half: it seems to me that a book about saying no would be incomplete without addressing **consent and the withholding of it as relates to sexy-time activities.**

So come for the mundane requests to switch seats or have parmesan cheese added to your pasta — stay for the discussion of why you are in no way obligated to put out, and how to convey that to anyone who thinks otherwise!

Permission to come aboard, Captain?

Back in the day, the minute a restaurant employee met me at the door and asked, "May I take your coat?" my people-pleasing instincts would take precedence over my low core temperature. I would agree to remove and relocate my outerwear because, variously:

What if the coat-check person is counting on those tips?

Is it rude to say no?

What if the manager doesn't like the look of jackets hanging over the backs of chairs if/when the clients finally get warm enough to remove them, and should that time come, the host will get in trouble if they didn't already convince me to relinquish mine?

Don't worry, I've since realized that these are ridiculous reasons to shiver through my shrimp cocktail. From "May I take your coat?" to "May I lick your toes now, Mistress?" the fact is: **inherent within a request by *anyone else* for permission to do anything to, with, or for *you* lies the built-in assumption that you might say no.**

It wouldn't hurt you to take them up on it every once in a while.

No-Tip: Say no to trick questions! Stay alert out there, people. If someone prefaces a request with "Do you mind if I…?" — and if you *do* mind — you have to say YES, not no. Don't get confused by subterfuge.

Sadly, I cannot travel back in time for a do-over and enjoy more fully the countless frigid meals I sat through in over–air conditioned restaurants before I understood that it was okay to say "No, I'd prefer to hang on to the only piece of fabric standing between me and a bout of hypothermia. I'll keep the scarf too, thanks."

But at least I can save you from a similar fate!

From requests to invade your personal space to those for taking more of your time or that upend expectations about how you thought this night was going — here are **a bunch of common requests for permission** and **Totally Legit Responses to them.**

REQUEST	TOTALLY LEGIT RESPONSE
"Would you like some freshly ground black pepper on that?"	"No thank you."
"Cute dog! Can I give him some treats?"	"I'd rather you didn't. Thanks for asking first!"
\<eager hotel bellhop reaches for your lone suitcase\>	"Oh, no, that won't be necessary. I've got wheels and I know how to use 'em."
"Can I get your phone number?"	"No."
"You've got something on the back of your dress. Should I brush it off for you?"	"Thanks, but I'll get it myself."

REQUEST	TOTALLY LEGIT RESPONSE
"Can I ask you a follow-up question?"	"Nope. We're done here."
"Can I bring a date to the wedding?"	"Unfortunately, we have to keep the guest list pretty tight."
"Will you switch seats with me?" (in general)	"I'd rather not."
"Will you switch seats with me?" (on an airplane)	"Sorry, I paid extra for the [window/aisle/exit row]."
"We couldn't get a sitter. Okay if the kids tag along to your dinner party?"	"Actually, we just got a Cards Against Humanity expansion pack we're itching to try out. Probably not appropriate for them. Bummer. We'll just invite you another time!"
"Can I just crash here tonight?"	"Um, no. I'll call you a Lyft."

When someone asks if they can bring a plus-one to your wedding or take your window seat, they are asking because they know full well that it is not automatically okay to just do those things. **If it** was AUTOMATICALLY OKAY, **they would not have felt the need to ASK PERMISSION in the first place.** That's how this works. Askers gonna ask. You are, however, free to drop a Hard No and proceed directly to your table.

It's chilly in here.

No means no

As you're well aware, I'm big on **setting boundaries**—i.e., making your intentions and preferences known—and on **enforcing boundaries**—i.e., warning of and doling out consequences to those who'd trespass into your OK corral. Indeed, I've harped upon boundaries throughout half of *Fuck No!* and for the entirety of *The Life-Changing Magic of Not Giving a Fuck*—and yet I'm just now realizing that I've never discussed them when it comes to, well, fucking.

My bad.

I could say that *The Life-Changing Magic of Not Giving a Fuck* was a sillier book for a sillier time, though that would be only half true. It was a deeply silly book. But the reality is that *all* time—forever ago and for every day to come—is very serious when it comes to having and not having sex for those who do and do not want to have it. It just so happens that today, as I write an equally silly book that I hope will be equally useful, more of us are talking more openly about setting and enforcing our **sexual boundaries** and it feels more urgent than ever to add my voice to the chorus.

Will it do any good? I don't know. I hope so. It certainly can't do any harm. So without further ado, I'm going to drop **the truthiest truth in** *Fuck No!* It does not get more truthy than this, folks.

Are you ready? Here's my hot take on sex and consent:

It doesn't matter if you're kissing, touching, stroking, rubbing, licking, humping, or penetrating; you name the frisky proposition, **the person on the receiving end should have the opportunity to indicate their acceptance** *before it commences* **and to pause or stop completely at any time.**

Furthermore, **consent to sex and sexual activity cannot be defined or understood as a mere** *lack* **of no.** It must be predicated on a clear, enthusiastic, and un-coerced yes — no ifs, ands, or surprise butt stuff about it.

As such, allow me to inform you — clearly and enthusiastically — that **you are entitled to say no to sex any time you can't, shouldn't, or don't want to have it (or keep having it).** For any reason. I've taken the liberty of creating a starter list of such reasons below, and you have my permission to add ANY OTHER GODDAMN REASON to it AT ANY TIME:

A PARTIAL LIST OF REASONS YOU'RE ENTITLED TO SAY NO TO SEX

Headache	It's Tuesday	_____
Stomachache	Anxious	_____
Sore knee	Sad	_____
Gotta pee	Busy	_____
Too tired	Dirty	_____
Too drunk	Not feelin' it	Etc.

And in a surprise twist: **YOU DON'T HAVE TO GIVE ANY REASON AT ALL!***

No means no. It always has and it always will. The more someone like me uses their modest platform and indefatigable typin' fingers to reassure someone like you of this fact, the more one hopes it will seep into the public consciousness and chip away at the utterly galling and wildly incorrect notion that any of us owe any others of us any kind of access to our bodies, *ever*.

While I have your attention, I have one more thing to say. This nugget goes out specifically to one of my anonymous survey responders, and also generally to everyone else on the planet:

Anybody who makes you feel OBLIGATED to have sex with them or GUILTY for not doing so is not someone who deserves to have sex with you.

You do not have to engage in the most intimate act imaginable just because the other participant in said act might get their fucking feelings hurt if you say no. *Game over. Thanks for playing! Try again never.*

You don't even have to do it if the person on the other end is actually being super cool about the whole thing and yet you still carry a sense of obligation and guilt *in your own mind* due to centuries of ass-backward cultural conditioning.

So lemme just say this a little louder for the people in the back:

---

* Not a twist.

OBLIGATION AND GUILT ARE NOT GOOD REASONS TO SAY YES TO SEX IF YOU CAN'T, SHOULDN'T, OR DON'T WANT TO HAVE IT. (OR KEEP HAVING IT.)

Right, I think we're done here. Good talk. Tell your friends and tip your bartenders!

WORK & OTHER
PROFESSIONAL
TRANSACTIONS

*bosses, clients, coworkers, customers,
and vendors, oh my!*

Switching gears for a bit from intimate relations to purely professional ones, let's tackle a subset of **no's that can affect your calendar and quality of life,** as well as your **career trajectory, your reputation,** and **your bank account.**

The declines in this chapter can be deployed from a corner office in Corporate America or from behind the bar at your local java joint. After all, a problem client is a problem client—whether they're attached to a six-figure account or a yappy Maltipoo that wants to drink from the staff watercooler.

I'll start with **vendors,** because whether you're the company's top saleswoman or a stay-at-home dad, you've got plenty to accomplish in any given day. **You don't need to be bogged down by *more* unwarranted, unproductive, or unwanted shit when you're off the clock.** Then I'll take you to the office and walk you through a variety of scenari-nos in which **coworkers, clients, and bosses might be asking too much of you** — and what you can say to keep them at bay.

Finally, I'll give you a quick tutorial on **saying no and resetting the bar in your favor** — be it with a prospective employer whose first offer isn't good enough, a landlord who's trying to raise your rent, or Mary Jo down at the flea market who can't wait to sell you one of her overpriced hand-knit fanny packs. Refusing invitations and declining to do favors may result in you having to do, spend, or otherwise exert yourself *less* — but **in a business context, saying no can also get you *more:*** such as money, autonomy, perks, or a two-for-one deal on belt bags. **Let's hear it for no-gotiating!**

Of course, my usual caveat applies: go ahead and say yes to any or all of this stuff if it makes sense to you — such as doing something a little outside your job description to prove to your boss that you have mad skillz, or giving a client a discount now to keep them coming back later.

But if you can't, shouldn't, or just don't want to — and **if the rewards of refusal far outweigh the risks of assent** — then it's a Pro No, bro.

Scenario-nos: vendors

I started easing you into this kind of thing way back in part I with sales-people and service industry folks. There, we focused on vendors offering you something (or something extra). Here, I want to challenge the ones who are trying to *take away from* or otherwise *do something to* you.

Instead of saying "I don't want that thing" before it's upon you, you'll be saying "I will not accept that thing" when it already is — a small but significant difference in terms of gathering confidence and asserting yourself under pressure.

Below, a few situations in which you may wish to take no shit from nobody and issue an N-to-tha-O:

- If your **PHONE PROVIDER** tries to raise prices when your contract is up for renewal, say **"I've been a customer in good standing for X years and I'm not prepared to continue at a higher rate."** This could definitely get you re-upped for no additional charge. (Been there, done that more than once.)

- If your **CREDIT CARD COMPANY** tells you they can-celed your card for suspected fraud and can't ship you a new one for three to five business days, say **"I'm afraid I need you to do better. For 15% APR, surely you can FedEx it over-night."** (Been here and done this too. Fucking hackers.)

- If your **PERSONAL TRAINER** adds another weight to the bar despite your protests, say **"I know I pay you to push my**

limits, but this is where they end." You may also wish to remind them that if *you* throw out your back, *they'll* be out of a job for six to eight weeks.

- If your **DOCTOR** tries to usher you in and out of your appointment in less time than it took for your ungrateful feral rescue cat to break one of the tiny bones in your hand, say **"Excuse me, but I'm not quite ready to leave until I fully understand everything we've discussed today."** It could be the difference between getting your co-pay's worth or going home with an insufficient understanding of how long it's going to take your fifth metacarpal to heal and what you could be doing to help it along. Not that Mister Stussy or I would know anything about that.

This all seems do-able, right? (At the very least it's try-able. Lemme know how it goes.)

Continuing up the loosely metaphorical ladder that provides the structure of this chapter, let's clamber on to **coworkers.** You still shouldn't be taking any shit, but you might need to be more subtle or less confrontational about it if you don't want trouble—or for your lunch to go mysteriously missing from the communal fridge.

Scenari-nos: coworkers

Guys. GUYS. If my survey is any indication, you are *entirely* too busy doing other people's work. What is going on out there? You're like a one-person team of sled dogs dragging your colleagues over the finish line day in and day out—not to mention covering for their lazy, forgetful, and hungover asses when they can't make it in altogether. You're cleaning up after dirty birdies in the break room, running all the office errands, getting shafted on group bar tabs, and finding out a whole lot more about Cynthia's recurring UTIs than you ever wanted to know.

You (and Cynthia) need to work on that. Allow me to assist.

WHAT IF YOUR COWORKER...

- **Asks for help when what they really want is for you to just do the whole thing for them**

  "Honestly, I don't have time for this."

  "I'm a little crazed right now."

  OPTIONAL NO-AND-SWITCH:
  "No can do. Unless you can take X off my plate? Want to trade?"

- **Asks you to pick up their slack when they have to leave early for "family stuff" or "to let the dog out," because they know you don't have kids or pets or whatever and they think that means you don't have any reason to say no**

  "Yeah...no. I've been looking forward to my night off all week."

  "I have a hot date with *Luther*."

"Ugh, sorry you're in a bind. This is why I don't have [kids/pets]. Good luck!"

Asks if you can cover for them completely

"I wish I could, but I've got plans."

OPTIONAL NO-FOR-NOW:
"Not today, but with a little more notice I might be able help you out another time."

If they are a habitual no-ffender:

"Afraid I can't help you this time."

"Is it just me, or is this becoming a pattern?"

"No, sorry."

If it's because they're too hungover to come in:

"Oof. No, but I'll drink a Gatorade Cool Blue today in your honor. Good luck out there!"

- **Inserts themselves in your work when you don't need or want them to**

  "No thank you, I can handle it."

- **Asks if you want to get together outside of work**

  "Not tonight, but thanks!"

"Alas, I have other plans."

"I appreciate the offer but I miss my [partner/futon/turtle]."

- **Asks you to go to networking events so they don't have to go alone:**

  "No thanks. I hate that shit."

- **Asks you to weigh in on their personal life**

  "I'd rather not talk about that kind of thing at the office."

  OPTIONAL NO-AND-SWITCH:
  "This seems like a conversation better suited to happy hour. If you're buying two-for-one margaritas, I'm all ears."

- **Asks you for a ride to/from work too often**

  "I wish I could keep helping you out, but to be honest the [travel time/gas/etc.] is getting to be too much for me."

- **Asks if they can bum a smoke all the time instead of buying their own**

  You should both quit. Smoking is really bad for you.

- **Asks you to organize gifts for other colleagues' birthdays, weddings, and babies and sticks you with the bill *every single* time**

"I'm happy to contribute but I'd rather not be the banker anymore."

Or if you're not able to contribute at all:

"I'm strapped right now and I can't afford to wind up holding the gift bag, so to speak. Can you run point this time? Thanks!"

- **Asks you to take the tedious, boring, and/or invisible part of the workload so they can have the interesting, fun, and/or credit-worthy part for themselves**

  "I'd prefer to divide things up differently. Here's how."

- **Asks you to participate in a photo shoot for ass-firming cream because they couldn't get any models to do it and the magazine you work for goes to press next week**

  "Fuck no!"

  OPTIONAL PRO NO:
  "Thank you for thinking of me for this opportunity. I'm flattered that you believe my bottom worthy of exhibition in a national print publication, but regrettably, I must decline."

Alright my little fucklings, we are churnin' and burnin'! Time to jump a rung to the **clients and customers** on whom you depend, in one form or another, to fund your employment.

Scenari-nos: clients and customers

Some of them are trying to take advantage of you; some are just clueless. Some of them have no boundaries or don't respect yours. And too many let their kids ransack the toy section like a crackhead looking for the last rock and expect *you* to clean it up.

Still, if you really need the job they're paying you for—whether directly, as with a client, or indirectly, if you're in the customer service industry—you will more than occasionally have to swallow your annoyance and just do whatever they ask. **This is called "being an adult."**

But you can **set boundaries,** like you might with a coworker, and **expectations,** like a boss sets for an employee. And the next time some guy at the gym you work in asks if you can "take care of that" nasty towel he tried to bank shot into the laundry bin and missed— keep in mind that **as long as you're willing to risk the consequences, you can actually do whatever the fuck you want.**

Pick it up yourself, LeBron.

WHAT IF YOUR CLIENT/CUSTOMER . . .

- **Asks for too many changes at the last minute**

   "Unfortunately, that's not going to be possible in the time we have left."

OPTIONAL NO-FOR-NOW:
"I'm not going to be able to change direction at this stage, but after you see my draft we can discuss next steps."

● **Asks if you can do it for less**

After you quote them a price:

"No, that's as low as I can go and still be able to devote the time it takes to give you the result you're looking for."

"It won't be feasible for me to do it for less."

"No, but if you want to shop around, I understand."

After you've finished the job:

"Unfortunately, the work is complete and I've already come in on budget."

"I wish I could help you out, but I can't grant discounts after the fact."

● **Pitches you a job you just don't want**

"Thanks for thinking of me, but I don't think that's the perfect fit."

"I appreciate the offer, but I'm not available." (The "at that price," "in that timeframe," or "to work with a known cheesedick" remains implied.)

- **Blurs the line between client and friend**

  If you are friends:

  "I'm sorry, but the only way this works for me is if I treat you like I treat all my clients."

  If you aren't friends, and don't want to be:

  "I'd prefer to keep this professional."

- **Asks for special treatment**

  "If I did it for you, I'd have to do it for all of my [clients/customers], and then I'd be out of a job."

  "My boss would very much frown upon that."

  "I respect your game, but that's a no-can-do."

  "I love you, Aunt Kelly, but Sunday is my day off. I'd be happy to wax your upper lip during regular salon hours."

ADD OPTIONAL SMILES, LAUGHS, WINKS, AND/ OR KNOWING NODS.

Oh *hell* no.

If someone — anyone — asks you to lie or cheat for them in a business context, SAY NO. Why would you ever say yes to putting your reputation and possibly your entire career and livelihood on the line? If your coworker asks you to punch out for them so they can leave an hour early undetected: *Sorry, I can't risk getting in trouble.* If a client asks you to work under the table so they don't have to pay the full price quoted by your company: *No, I'm not allowed to do that.* If your manager asks you to tell his wife you were with him on his recent "business" trip to Puerto Vallarta: *I don't want any part of this, Dave.*

And if you're struggling with a response, just replace the "ask" in your mind with the specific ramifications of your coworker/client/ Dave's request, i.e., **"Hey, will you put your reputation and possibly your entire career and livelihood on the line for me?"** If that doesn't get you to *Hell no* faster than Mrs. Dave can dial up her divorce lawyer, I don't know what will.

Speaking of Dave, before we take this shit straight to the top, I should touch on an aspect of officially opting out that can be especially anxiety inducing for one Yes-Man in particular.

I wouldn't say I was *missing* it: FOMO at work

The office is treacherous no'ing ground for all of us. Overachievers, for obvious reasons. Pushovers can't stand up for themselves in general, so why would they be any better at it in the face of authority? People-Pleasers may have bosses, employees, colleagues, *and* clients to kowtow to: it adds up, but no more than family + friends + tourists asking you to take their picture when you're in a hurry.

Those folks' hang-ups are relatively similar whether at work or at play, and I've put forward the core coping strategies already — with lessons on valuing your time/energy/money, setting boundaries, recognizing short-term vs. long-term "ease" and warranted vs. unwarranted guilt, and learning to say *Sorry, NotSorry.*

Then there are the FOMO'ers.

As you'll recall from the INVITATIONS chapter, **FOMO boils down to anxiety — over making a decision, and whether it was the right one in hindsight.** And in some ways, professional FOMO is similar to funtime FOMO:

- Like introverts who wonder if there's something wrong with them for turning down party invites, workplace FOMO'ers may be insecure about their level — and lack of — ambition. (*Should I want this more? Is there something wrong with me that I don't?*)

- Or they're comfortable with their own *desire* to say no, but don't necessarily trust that they're making the right decision. (*Am I being short-sighted? Am I going to regret this?*)

I mentioned earlier that I don't tend to experience the fear of missing out in social situations; I have a clear notion of what "fun" is worth to me in relation to "relaxing alone with a book and not having to put on makeup" and I don't give a fuck about what anyone thinks of me in those terms. And I would argue that getting to this place with regard to one's professional FOMO requires the same logic, reasoning, and weighing of consequences that we talked about already: **having confidence in WHO YOU ARE and WHAT YOU WANT.**

But I also acknowledge that **FOMO isn't all fun and Instagram likes.**

The stakes are higher when your livelihood is on the line, and **you also need the confidence to TAKE CALCULATED RISKS —** especially when you're worried you might get unfairly penalized by an unhappy boss, client, or business partner for saying no. (*Should I just give in? Are THEY going to make me regret this?*)

When it comes to my professional life, my resolve to say no has been known to falter. (Why Yes/When No? Because: Money! Security! Money!) I'm getting better at valuing my time and energy against whatever compensation I'm offered in exchange, and demanding more. But that still lands me at yes — often to things I don't really want to do — because **FOMO tells me if I say no altogether, I may lose the chance to even *make* those valuations in the future.**

Opportunity knocks but once, right?

WRONG.

Yes, there are once-in-a-lifetime opportunities, like seeing Halley's Comet or the L.A. Clippers make it to the finals, and then there's everything else. So I'll tell you what I tell myself when FOMO starts whispering in my ear.

If you're happy with what you've got, *stay happy* and *say no*. A Pro No will get you off the hook, and respectably so.

If you're happy *now* but still have your eye on *later,* No-for-Now keeps doors open and opportunities a-knockin'.

And if doing what's *right* for you rubs other people the *wrong* way, then, in the immortal words of Baseball Hall of Famer Dennis Eckersley: Fuck 'em.

With that, it's onward and upward to our topmost rung: the Realm of Dave.

Up, up, and no way!

Several years ago, my then-boss* asked me if I would like to represent the company on a transatlantic business trip. **My inner Yes-Men leapt to attention.** The Overachiever was flattered to have been

---

* Nice guy, not Puerto Vallarta Dave.

asked first among my colleagues and tempted to add another feather to my already overfull cap. The People-Pleaser worried that my boss would be disappointed if I turned down his offer. Little Miss FOMO cautioned that if I said no, the forgone opportunity might haunt me for the rest of my career.

And yet... I didn't *want* to go. Not even a little bit.

First and foremost, I hate flying — so many lines, germs, uncomfortable seats, and humans on their absolute worst behavior. I'll endure it in service of a fun vacation, but at the time I didn't relish the idea of showing up to work my day job in a distant city with a crick in my neck and a head cold I caught from the toddler in 7C.

I'm also not a huge fan of enforced schmoozing, which would have been a major component of this endeavor. Plus, I knew that if I took a weeklong jaunt to London, I'd end up behind on my day-to-day tasks back home in New York, with jet lag to boot.

Every fiber of my being wanted to shout NO THANKS!

I'm not going to lie to you, though — I wasn't able to spit that out right away. I felt a shitload of pressure to say yes, and all of this took place long before I became an anti-guru and ninja of no. But I *really* hate flying, so instead (and presaging what would one day become a No-Tip in this very book), I begged a stay of execution: **"Thanks, I'll have to think about it!"**

A couple of days later my boss asked if I'd made a decision; he needed an answer because if I couldn't go, there were other colleagues vying for the opportunity. In a moment of either clarity or desperation (Have I mentioned how much I hate flying?), I took a deep breath and told him the truth:

No, no I did not want to go.

Initially he seemed shocked that I, his on-staff embodiment of Reese Witherspoon's character in *Election*, would turn down any opportunity to overachieve. I pressed on, sharing all of the totally reasonable reasons *why* I didn't want to go,* and concluded by saying that although I was very appreciative, I thought he should offer the trip to someone who would get just as much out of it and also certainly enjoy it more.

And you know what? HE WAS COOL ABOUT IT. He even said he sometimes wished *he* could say no to work travel, and that he totally respected my gangsta.

I mean, not in those words, but still.

What I learned from that ordeal was that **it's okay to protect our mental, emotional, and physical health by saying no to our bosses if we feel we need to and that it's realistic to do so.**

I mean, it's not like you show up at work every day to fuck around; otherwise they wouldn't call it "work," they'd call it "remunerative fun." You know what you're expected to do to earn your paycheck, and then if you're asked to do more — as I was in this situation — you can set and enforce boundaries as needed.

Sometimes it's worth the extra outlay of fuck bucks to be helpful or to make a good impression; **other times it clearly is not.** And "worth it" might mean "gaining favor, respect, or reward with your boss," but it could also mean "doing this thing I don't want and shouldn't have to do is still worth not getting punished or fired over *not* doing it." Figuring that out is up to you. Acting on it, I can help you with.

---

* In this case, to enumerate my reasons felt liberating.

The prospect of saying no to a boss can be scary. I've had a couple of superiors who were legit mean and one that was certifiably nutso. But for the most part they've all been pretty great — and more importantly, they have all been *human*. So is yours, which means they probably wish they could refuse their boss sometimes too.

When you proceed with that rational assumption in mind, it gets a little bit less scary, no?

And if you **relay your no in an honest, polite, professional way** — one hopes your boss will respect your gangsta. Perhaps even to the point of rewarding you for being honest, polite, and professional instead of punishing you for being an overachieving, people-pleasing wimp who doesn't know how to prioritize.

Scenari-nos: bosses

Too many of us are being asked by our superiors to stay late or come in on our days off, to take on tons of extra work for no extra pay, and to do things far outside our job descriptions — such as, in the case of one poor soul who responded to my survey, cleaning up the bar area their boss had "relations" on earlier that day.

Ew. That is fucked up in more ways than one.

And although I no longer report to anyone but me, in a gesture of solidarity I offer you the following no's with which to **minimize your stress, maximize your productivity, and neutralize your inclination to quit in a fit of rage** instead of just saying "Regrettably, that won't be possible. But I can tell you where we keep the towels."

WHAT IF YOUR BOSS . . .

- **Demands a too-short deadline**

   "That's not going to be possible."

   "To be honest, I feel like I can do it really quickly or really well, but not both. Which would you prefer?"

- **Asks you to stay late to do something**

   "I'm sorry, today isn't going to work for me."

   OPTIONAL NO-AND-SWITCH:
   "Today isn't going to work for me, but if it can wait, I'll definitely make time for it [tomorrow/later this week/next week]."

- **Invites you to socialize with them outside of work**

   "Thanks for the offer, but I can't make it."

- **Asks you to work on a day you were supposed to have off**

   "Unfortunately, I've already made plans that can't be changed."

   ADD OPTIONAL SPECIFICS:
   "My mother will absolutely murder me if I'm not home for her annual Arbor Day singalong."

- **Asks you to do a lot of additional work for no additional moolah**

    "I don't think it's right for me to continue taking on more responsibilities without being compensated for them. I hope you understand."

- **Repeatedly asks you to cover for a colleague who sucks**

    "I'm afraid I'm not going to be able to finish all of my own stuff on time if I take on any more of [colleague who sucks]'s work."

    "I don't love the fact that [colleague who sucks] puts me in this position on a regular basis. I'm hoping you can take this up with them directly so it stops impacting me [and the rest of the team]."

    OPTIONAL NO-FOR-NOW:
    "This situation of regularly covering for [colleague who sucks] is not really working for me. But if you're interested in combining our positions, I'd love to talk to you sometime about increasing my responsibilities along with a promotion and pay raise."

- **Asks for volunteers to serve on a committee**

  "I'd rather not, thank you."

  OPTIONAL POWER NO WHEN THE REQUEST IS DIRECTED AT A GROUP OF PEOPLE:
  <crickets>

- **Expects you to dog-sit their puppy at your desk all day**

  "I'm sorry, I'm allergic." (Even if you're not, this is an acceptable lie for a thoroughly unacceptable request. Dog people, sheesh. You don't see crazy cat ladies bringing their fur babies to the office. They keep 'em stacked all over the urine-scented patio furniture at home, where they belong.)

- **Asks you to do other things not in your job description**

  If it's something you don't know how to do:

  "I'd hate to disappoint you by doing it poorly; I think you should ask [insert appropriate coworker] to field this one."

  If it's something you shouldn't have to do:

  "I like to be a team player, but I have to tell you this doesn't feel like what I signed on for."

  If it's something you just don't want to do:

  "If there's any way you can ask someone else to handle that, I'd appreciate it."

RELATED: If your boss is the kind of person who expects you to clean up after their afternoon delights, they might also be the kind of person who won't take no for an answer. **Ready your flowchart! What are the consequences of saying no?** Are they worse than using a bar towel to wipe out the wet spot? If so, are you prepared to face them?

I can't decide for you, but I will say that calling in an anonymous tip to the Health Department can be a satisfying way to wind down after a long day's work.

Dr. No

Ooh, look, here's another one of those instructive personal anecdotes I like to throw in when the time is right.

In college, one of my professors hired me to be her research assistant. I imagined the job would entail spending hours each week photocopying and collating in a dank library basement, and forsooth, this was how it began.

Then one day when I was delivering some papers to her house, she asked me to go down the ramshackle stairs to her basement to move her clothes from the washer to the dryer. She had a bad hip and I was there already, so I said okay.

Another time, she gave me her ATM PIN and asked me to take out a couple hundred dollars in cash for her. My Spidey senses pinged with each press of the button on the bank machine pad, nervous that if she ever misplaced twenty dollars she'd immediately assume I stole it from her — and she was rather…disorganized…so this scenario did not seem out of the question.

But I did it. *Just this once,* I figured, *and if she asks again, I'll tell her I don't feel right about it.*

The next time I went to her house, Ol' Creaky Hips directed me up a ladder to dust off her bookshelves while she watched. *Hmm.* When I finished doing that, she asked me to empty her dishwasher. I was getting a little tired of playing Cinderella, but I needed the money and it's not like slotting wineglasses into a cupboard is hard labor. When I opened said dishwasher and found not stemware on the top rack, but a row of silicone sex toys, I realized my error in judgment.

I quit via email that evening. I don't remember if I ever even told my parents, but I did SAY I had told my parents and that they "had concerns" about this job "not being what I signed on for."

Scapegoats, for the win!

What if YOU'RE the boss?

Since bosses occupy positions of authority that make it inherently easier for them to say no, I didn't exactly write this book with CEOs in mind. But I have managed employees in my day, and I know it can be complicated to deal with the wants, needs, and mistakes of those below you in the pecking order and for whom you are responsible. Especially if you have a people-pleasing streak you haven't been able to shake since your own days low on the pole.

For example, if you run a retail company, staff members may

request holidays off that you **CAN'T** grant because your business thrives on summer tourism or Christmas shoppers. It's up to you to **deliver the no-can-do in a polite but firm way.**

And Glen from Marketing seems like a nice enough guy, but he averages about three fuckups a week and he doesn't seem to be learning from any them. As the boss, your bottom line is only as good as the mediocrity you tolerate, so someday Glen's going to beg for leniency (again) and you **SHOULDN'T** give it to him — **or else you'll be setting a costly precedent for your whole team.**

Oh, and your assistant is lusting after a promotion that would take her off your staff and into the higher echelons of the company. Even though she deserves it, you **JUST DON'T WANT TO** lose her *and* have to look for someone new right now. (**This is your prerogative,** just like it's hers to give two weeks' notice if she gets a better offer elsewhere.)

What's a *jefe* to do?

I submit that if you're the boss and you're having trouble doling out no's, **there are plenty of ways to do so without going all Queen of Dragons on your employees.**

In addition to a standard Pro No, the **No-and-Switch and the No-for-Now are great options** for staff seeking time off ("I can't give you Christmas, but you can have a four-day weekend in January") or assistants seeking upward mobility ("Now is not an ideal time for me to lose you *and* have to look for a replacement, but if you find me some great candidates, I'll interview them.")

And when Glen walks in all sheepish-like the morning after his latest subpar presentation and asks you to give him his fourth second chance this week, **Glen gets the Hard No.**

(Honestly, if letting go of a guy who costs you more than he earns in commissions keeps you up at night, you may not be cut out for this whole management thing.)

Now that we've taken in the view from the top, it's time to make a lateral move into a skill that bosses, employees, vendors, *and* clients will find useful: **negotiating.**

At the beginning of this chapter, we guarded against you getting shafted — such as when a doctor tries to shuffle you out too quickly or T-Mobile tries to gouge you too deeply.

As a bookend, I want to show you **how to gain even *more* in certain situations by saying a well-timed, well-executed no.**

The power of no-gotiation

For example, say your lease is up and your landlord presents you with a rent increase for next year. It's obvious that you don't WANT to pay more for the privilege of living in the same place. You also don't want to physically move, nor take on the expense and hassle of the process. But if you say no to paying more, your landlord might tell you that's too bad, guess you'll have to vacate by the end of the month.

Here's when you run through your *Must I? Should I? Will I?* exercises to ascertain whether you HAVE TO pony up to keep the place, and whether you're WILLING to do so. Good job, and I appreciate you taking my flowchart to heart.

Now it's time to take it *to the next level:*

- Ask not only what the consequences might be for YOU to say no, but what the consequences would be for the other party.

- Why do they want what you have (e.g., money or labor), and how badly do they need it?

- Identify your risk and reward, and then identify theirs too.

To show you what I mean, let's inhabit your landlord's mind-set for a hot sec. Finding new *tenants* is a hassle too. And if the timing doesn't work out just right, a couple weeks' or months' rent could dissolve while the apartment lies empty. You know what you're paying, so you know exactly how much that is, and the total doesn't look too appetizing from either side.

> If you say **"I'd love to stay, but I can't afford that,"** it's possible they'll do their own risk/reward calculations and re-up your lease with no increase.

> It's also possible they'll respond **"Sorry kid, I've got bills to pay. The monthly goes up or you get out!"** (I don't know why your landlord talks like a 1940s gangster, but to each his own.)

Back to your options and their consequences. Paying more for the same place isn't ideal... but what if it's an *improved* place?

> You might say **"I'm not sure the apartment is worth it to me in its current condition at a higher price. But if you'll make X, Y, and Z improvements, then I'd be happy to re-sign."**

In your landlord's view, a one-time cash outlay for a new toilet and a nice set of blinds could be worth a stable tenant who's essentially willing to pay back that investment over the course of the year, and they'll say **"You've got yourself a deal, Charlie!"** (Your name is not Charlie.)

Or you could just go ahead and call Mr. Roper's bluff.

The Walkaway

If you're willing and able, you can *always* negotiate down from your ideal position. But if you're in the mood to take a risk, you could also walk away entirely. Say something like, "No problem, I understand. It seems we've reached the end of our time together. Have a good day!" And then see what happens. If the other party in this negotiation needs what you have that badly, they may very well shout, "Hold on a minute there, tough guy! You drive a hard bargain, but I like your style" at your receding back. (Full disclosure: I didn't invent the Walkaway, but if this is the first you're hearing about it, I'm happy to take credit. Then we both get something out of the deal.)

No-gotiating works in all kinds of scenarios, cash-based and otherwise. Here are a few more ways to reap what you no:

- **Got assigned to a project or a client you don't like?**

  Speak up. Approach your boss honestly and politely with your misgivings. Say, "I don't really want to work [on this/with them]—and here's why." Use it as an chance to pitch yourself to the mission or team you prefer. Whether you're already a middle manager or just starting out as an intern, trust me, nobody has given your career trajectory nearly as much thought as YOU have. And if you can drill your objections and objectives down to a persuasive presentation, you could be saying sayonara to an undesirable assignment and hello to the department of your dreams.

- **Got a job offer that isn't good enough?**

Turn it down by explaining that you'd love to take advantage of this opportunity, but the salary is too low for you to leave your current job. You can even offer them a target number — a No-and-Switch — and see what happens. (Aim high so you have room to negotiate down to something that works for both parties.)

If they say they've reached their limit, well then, you don't have to take a job you couldn't really afford to take anyway. But if they come back with a salary bump or commission increase, you just no'd your way to a nice raise. Drinks on you!

Or maybe they won't budge on the money, but you still want out of your current sitch and/or into this one. You could say "The salary is just too low for me to accept your offer as-is. What can you do for me in terms of a title promotion?" Assistant vs. Associate Manager may or may not mean much to you, but if they'll do it, a better title puts you in a better position the *next time* you go on the market. Food for thought.

- **Got offered a promotion you don't want?**

  Not everybody's itching to make the move from bartender to bar manager or floor sales to head office. If you covet neither the different vibe nor the added stress that comes with added responsibility, it's okay to say no. Someone else gets a chance to move up the ladder and you preserve your quality of life. Not all gains are measured in the words on a business card or the decimal numbers on a paycheck.

FuckNotes: Business Edition

Remember your training in advance no-tice from page 145? Those tips come in handy here too: do not reply right away, don't be an asshole, and keep it brief. Get the Pro No's flowing with the following:

- A polite salutation (i.e., "Dear Jim" or "Good morning")
- The thing you've been offered or asked to do
- A reason why you can't/shouldn't do it (optional)
- Phrase describing the completion of the offer/task (e.g., "squared away," "taken care of," "sorted out")
- A polite closing (e.g., "Sincerely" or "Regards")

If you CAN'T

_____,
polite salutation

Unfortunately, _____ won't be possi-
*whatever you've been
offered/asked to do*

ble for me [because_____]. [Add
reason why you can't

optional No-and-Switch or No-for-Now]

_____,
polite closing

_____
your name

If you SHOULDN'T

_____,
polite salutation

Unfortunately, _____ won't be possible
*whatever you've been
offered/asked to do*

for me [because _____]. I'm sorry I
optional reason why

couldn't be of more assistance on this one,

but I wish you all the best in getting this

_____.
phrase describing completion

_____*,*
   polite closing

_____
   your name

If you JUST DON'T WANT TO

_____*,*
   polite salutation

Unfortunately, _____ won't be possi-
                whatever you've been
                offered/asked to do

ble. I'm sorry I couldn't be of more assistance

on this one, but I wish you all the best in

getting this _____.
           phrase describing completion

_____*,*
   polite closing

_____
   your name

PARTNERS

sex, money, communication, division of labor, and back waxing

We've been diligently working our way from people you don't know, like, or care about to those you kind of have to care about in order to get shit done or make a living. And now we're getting to those **you care a great deal about, and voluntarily so.** Whether you have, had, and/or expect to have **a romantic partner** again someday, you know that such relationships come with requests and expectations beyond and different from those of bosses, coworkers, friends, or roommates.

For example: "Do you want to raise our kids Catholic?" Or: "Can I interest you in Reverse Cowgirl?"

When you're intimate with someone — living, sleeping, sexing, eating, pet-owning, co-parenting — **it might seem like you have no boundaries left.** Or that there can't or shouldn't *be* any boundaries, because what's love if not granting another person the key to your heart and your Gates of Hell No?

Whoa there, partner, hold your sheep! **ALL relationships thrive**

on normal, healthy boundaries. From mutual financial decisions to non-mutual interests, shared tasks, and gross asks, in this chapter we'll explore a variety of situations in which you must, should, or want to say no to your boo — and then how to do it without unconsciously uncoupling.

(Unless uncoupling is the goal. I'll touch on that, too.)

Scenari-nos: partners

They say the two biggest strains on any romantic relationship are **money and sex.** I'm no accredited couples therapist, but my survey results indicate that I should expand these pressures to include **career stuff, emotional and physical labor, criticism,** and **in-law management** (if applicable).

But first and foremost, although couples who go on HGTV home renovation shows would lead you to believe it's double sinks in the master bath, **the true key to a successful relationship is good communication.**

We'll start there, since there's no satisfaction in dropping the mic if it's not even on.

He said, she said, they said, we said

In the beginning, you need to communicate about whether or not you even *are* a "couple," so let's open with a status check:

WHAT IF THE ANSWER IS NO WHEN YOUR SIGNIFICANT OTHER....

- **Asks if you want to be exclusive or call each other boyfriend-girlfriend or whatever the kids are doing these days**

  "No, that's not really what I'm looking for."

OPTIONAL NO-FOR-NOW:

"I'm not sure I'm ready to have that conversation. Let's see how things go over the next few [weeks/months] and then maybe we can talk about it again?"

"I'm not there yet, but that doesn't mean I won't be."

- **Asks if you want to move in together**

  "No, I'm happy with the way things are for now."

  "I need some time to think about that."

  "I like to have my own separate space to go back to, but I can see a day coming when I'll be ready to take the plunge."

- **Asks you to get back together after a breakup**

  "That's not going to happen."

  "I feel like our relationship ended where and when it needed to."

  "No thanks, I'm good."

- **Asks you to marry them**

Life isn't all rom-coms and Nicholas Sparks novels. For every viral proposal video there's a couple out there that just isn't meant to be, and perhaps only one of them knows it. If you find yourself in one of these lopsided relationships — or even one that might *someday* turn matrimonial but that day is not, to your mind, *right now* or even *anytime soon*—

Do not say yes just because you don't want to hurt your partner's feelings. (It will hurt them more if you change your mind tomorrow or call off the wedding next year or doom them to a sham marriage and eventual divorce.)

Do not say yes just because you're caught off guard and you'd like to think about this but you're not sure you're "allowed" to. (You are.)

Do not say yes just because you're afraid if you turn them down you'll have blown your one chance of getting married at all, even though you don't want to marry *this* person. (FOMO is the absolute worst reason to get engaged, followed closely by "needing a new set of nonstick pans.")

Say No, say Not right now, say I need to think about this— but for the love of all that is old, new, borrowed, and blue: DO NOT SAY YES.

Now, assuming you remain coupled—engaged, married, living in sin, or otherwise—your communication skills will continue to evolve. From going out too many nights a week to hosting too many poker games to using your spare room as a home for wayward fraternity buddies, **how do you say no, be heard, and stand firm without**

creating conflict (or at least more conflict than is strictly necessary)?*

The answer is: **keep it simple.**

	NOPE.	I'M NOT FEELING IT TODAY.	THAT'S NOT REALLY MY THING.	NEVER.
DO YOU WANT TO GO OUT?				
DO YOU WANT TO HAVE PEOPLE OVER?				
DO YOU WANT TO HANG OUT WITH [PERSON/PEOPLE YOU DON'T LIKE]?				
DO YOU WANT TO [DO A SPECIFIC ACTIVITY]?				
DO YOU WANT TO [DO SOMETHING YOU'RE AFRAID OF]?				
DO YOU WANT TO [TRY THIS THING YOU HAVE NEVER DONE BUT KNOW YOU WON'T LIKE]?				

---

* If you and your significant other get off on conflict, you can skip this section and go piss off and resent each other to your hearts' content. Enjoy the makeup sex!

You needn't launch into a song-and-dance routine about why you don't want to do karaoke with his coworkers or go to a rave with her roommates. (That would, in fact, defeat the entire purpose.) Instead, consult the chart on the previous page, similar to the one on page 119, and deliver the appropriate no.

Is there something to be said for **stretching outside your comfort zone** to have an adventure that may turn out to be fun and exhilarating? And for **doing something that is meaningful for your partner** (and not especially painful/terrifying for you) even if you wouldn't otherwise choose to do it?

Sure there is. Why do you think I agreed to see *The Matrix Reloaded* on opening weekend in New York City?

But there's also something to be said for not having to clean up after your third impromptu late-night party of the month or spending your weekend in the E.R. due to an entirely predictable paddleboarding mishap. Your lady friend is not coordinated enough to join you in this activity. You both know this.

Happy couples don't necessarily have to do everything together, nor want to do all the same things. All they really have to do **is communicate and respect each other's choices**.

My husband and I are living proof that a hermit can hook up with a social butterfly and have a mutually satisfying social life. We do what we both want to do together, but I also "let" him

---

Things your significant other might enjoy that you might not

Live sporting events
Televised sporting events
Reggae shows
Church stuff
Camping
Eating Korean BBQ

---

go out without me and he "lets" me stay home without him.

Sometimes the question isn't "Do you want to go?" but rather "Do you mind if I do?"

If the answer is no on both counts, then you're good to go — or to stay home with a jar of peanut butter and a sleeve of Ritz crackers. (Fine, two sleeves.)

> **Things your significant other is free to enjoy without you**
>
> Live sporting events
> Televised sporting events
> Reggae shows
> Church stuff
> Camping
> Eating Korean BBQ

You da real MVP

A system that's worked well in my relationship for nigh on two decades — with the exception of one awesome chair with a royal blue velvet cushion that my husband totally should have let me buy at the Brooklyn Flea in 2008 — is called **Mutual Veto Power (MVP).**

The way it works is that if either of us comes out flatly against something, like, say, wicker as a general decorating concept, we've pre-agreed that there will be no protracted whining about and/or blatant disregard for that opinion. **One "no" vote is enough to take wicker off the table.**

(We developed MVP after he told me he didn't want a pet and I hounded him to go see a refrigerator box full of kittens in Soho and we ended up with twelve years of Doug, the Worst Cat Ever.)*

---

* Okay, technically we ended up with two more cats in the Dominican Republic last year, but in my defense, I'd never fed a stray cat before and I didn't know that if you feed them once or twice YOU HAVE TWO MORE CATS MEOW.

7 more things you and your partner may disagree about for which MVP comes in handy

Paint colors
China patterns
Large expenditures
Wall hangings
Theme parties
Lawn ornaments
Swinging

On the flip side, if one of us is merely neutral on a purchase, vacation destination, activity, or whatnot—and the other really wants it—the neutral party doesn't stand in the way. The result is that **at least one of us is getting what we want much of the time, and *neither* of us are getting what we *don't* want.**

Obviously if the subject is of significant import, such as whether or not to have children or which is the correct way to load a roll of toilet paper, a larger conversation and/or some light arm wrestling may be warranted. But generally speaking, **MVP is an efficient way to dispense with minor quibbles that don't merit major conflict.** For example:

"Do you like these curtains?"

"No."

"Do you want to honeymoon in Japan?"

"No."

"Can we do a joint Ina and Jeffrey costume for Halloween?

"No."

To-do or not to-do, that is the question

I'm of the belief that household chores — like taking out the trash, vacuuming, laundry, or doing the dishes — should be split as evenly as possible among partners who share a domicile, on the understanding that some of us have different strengths, preferences, and/or a lot more (or less) time on our hands, and that part of being in a relationship is working this shit out amongst ourselves.

Of course, some partners occupy different homes — each to their own pile of dirty dishes in the sink — but either way, **we all wind up taking on "chores" on behalf of the couple**: planning get-togethers or shopping for gifts or booking appointments with the real estate agent to look for apartments in which we might one day share a sink of dirty dishes. And whenever the labor division feels unbalanced, you may want to take it upon yourself to right the scales.

WHAT IF YOUR PARTNER . . .

● **Asks you to send the email**

"I'm pretty busy right now. Think you could field this one?"

"Actually, can you pass on the Settlers of Catan tournament for us? Mara and Gustav are your friends. Thanks!"

● **Asks you to make the appointment**

"It would be better for me if you can be the one to set this up."

"I dealt with the electrician last week. If you could do the plumber now, that'd be great."

- **Asks you to organize the group outing**

  "I'm a little burnt out on troop-rallying at the moment. Think you could get this ball rolling?"

  OPTIONAL NO-AND-SWITCH:
  "I don't have the bandwidth to get twelve people to agree on a restaurant, but I'm happy to invite them all here for Domino's if you prefer. Unless you want to handle it?"

- **Asks you to shop for the gifts**

  "I've been thinking that we should divide gift-shopping duties more evenly since I tend to do all of it. Let's start now."

  "So, a home breathalyzer kit for your uncle and a muzzle for your mom, then?"

- **Asks you to make dinner (or do anything else, every time) because you're "better at it"**

  "Ah, that's only because practice makes perfect. No time like the present to start learning a new skill!"*

---

* Does not apply to Aperol spritzes, which no amount of training could ever result in me making better than my husband does. This is the fizzy, slightly bitter hill I will die on.

It's also possible that **your partner isn't so much *asking* you to do things** like take out the trash or buy all the Hanukkah gifts for the grandkids, but rather that **it's always been assumed you would handle this kind of stuff**; or maybe they asked you to do it once, you said yes, and it **somehow turned into a permanent thing.**

If you want to rewrite the shared to-do list, you'll need to marshal one of those **Proactive No's** I mentioned on page 69 in the form of a preemptive directive of your own. Here are a couple of solid lead-ins:

> "Can I talk to you about something? I don't love being the one to do X all the time, so I'd like to come up with a plan for making it a bit more equal in the future."

> "So, I've been thinking that X is usually my job and Y is yours, but maybe we could switch it up for a while and see how it goes? Variety is the spice of life!"

Honey, have you seen the tweezers?

There's the boundless intimacy of true love, and then there's popping someone else's zits. If you and your pookie-pie are mutually content to hunker down for the evening and forage for blackheads or pluck back hair or bleach each other's naughty holes, then keep on truckin': I wish you a lifetime of happiness. But just know that it's AOK to say *No way, José* when someone you're casually boning, seriously dating, or engaged or married to asks you to perform an unpleasant act or come take a look at the prize-winning log they just

---

left in the flume. If your love is pure, it should be able to withstand a Hard No for gross and/or grossly inappropriate requests. I'm going to go out on a limb and say there are plenty of qualified aestheticians and fetish websites that can field this one.

Hey, while you're up...?

When my husband had shoulder surgery, I hauled ten-pound bags of ice back and forth from the deli to our apartment to feed the cold therapy machine he was hooked up to for two weeks. When my stupid feral trash cat inadvertently broke my left hand, the hubs helped me shave my right armpit for a month.

We all do what we gotta do.

And when your partner asks you to grab something from the other room or ferry their glass to the sink or check the fridge to see if we have any more mini Snickers bars because you're already up and they're about to start their period and have a sudden visceral need for chocolate-covered caramel, peanuts, and nougat, you may be happy to say *Sure,* or *No problem,* or *I guess I'm going to the grocery store now.*

But if you were not already up and/or you find your good nature being exploited a little too regularly when you are — a Hard No could help reset the relationship dynamics. Just sayin'.

REQUEST	RESPONSE
"Can you get me my glasses?"	"Can you not see where they are?"
"Can you go check to see if the door is locked?"	"I'm willing to live dangerously tonight."
"Can you walk the dog?"	"He told me he prefers your company."

Maybe you shouldn't be doing that

More than a few people responded to my survey saying **they wished they could say no to partners making inherently critical requests** — such as that they not do or wear or eat certain things, or hang out with certain people.

Well.

Again, I'm no Chuck Woolery, but it seems to me that it's hard to have a love connection with someone who is constantly asking you to behave differently or change fundamental things about yourself.

And I'm not talking about an other half who asks you to stop drinking so much because they're worried you have a serious health problem, or one who we can all agree is objectively correct when they say you ought to retire those well-worn Camp Beaver View shorts from 1992. At this point they're a little too on the nose.

I'm talking about a husband, wife, BF, GF, or gender noncon-forming partner who suggests that you go to the gym to **"take care**

of that holiday weight you put on," or who frequently asks that you stop doing inoffensive stuff that you enjoy, like singing in public or skipping down the street. Or wearing knee-high athletic socks with shorts when you're nowhere near a soccer field. Weirdo.

If this is a familiar pattern in your relationship, it may not be possible (or advisable) to try to salvage things with someone who seems decidedly not that into what makes you, *you*. I'm sorry, I know that's not much fun to contemplate. But on the bright side, maybe your main squeeze honestly doesn't realize the impact their comments and requests are having on you — and **you might be able to open their eyes to your perspective if you have the courage to tell them.**

If I were you, I wouldn't wait.

Case in point: My high school boyfriend never made negative comments about my weight and always told me I was beautiful, but we each had our own body image issues and prom season was fast approaching, so we were trying to keep fit as a couple. One afternoon as we stood together after class, I mentioned I was jonesing for Pizza Hut. He smiled and poked me in the belly as if to say "Are you sure that's a good idea?"

In the moment, I understood that he thought he was making a joke, but I also felt like I'd been punched in the gut with a lead breadstick. I still remember that feeling. I even remember the teal blue, scooped-neck GAP t-shirt I was wearing as I looked down at his forefinger lightly pressing into the fabric. I don't remember what I said to him in response — probably because I internalized the shock, shame, and sadness, pretended it was okay, and said nothing at all.

Given that I'm still thinking about it twenty-three years later, this was probably not the best course of action.

Today, and with the hindsight of several more relationships and a lot of personal development under my ever-expanding belt, I would have told him, "I'm sure you didn't mean anything by it, but that just made me feel really bad. Please don't do it again."

So now I'm telling YOU: **if someone you love makes you feel bad about yourself, you should speak up, push back, and say** *No, I'm not cool with that, and here's why.*

If you can do that—and if they're willing to listen, apologize, and learn—you might just have a personal pan keeper on your hands.

It's all about the Benjamins (and the nookie)

We now commence our prime-time programming: **money and sex.**

Conflict over either of these can torpedo a relationship faster than an unexplained Visa charge from Larry Flynt's Barely Legal on Bourbon Street, and it'll be up to you and your paramour to decide how far you can go to accommodate one another when the road gets bumpy. If you've been dating for thirty days, the answers might be different than if you've been married for thirty years, but **here are some general ways to voice your objections when you disagree on the fundamentals of sharing expenses and/or orgasms:**

- **On spending (dinners, trips, etc.) that's out of your budget**

    "If it's all the same to you, I'd rather not. I'm feeling the burn on expenses lately."

"Sounds great, but honestly I/we can't afford that right now."

"We've been doing a lot of [expensive thing] and I think I/we should probably tighten ye olde purse strings for a while."

OPTIONAL NO-AND-SWITCH:
"That feels like too big a stretch, but how about we [do/buy/go to] [a cheaper version]?"

If they insist on paying and you feel uncomfortable about that (FOR ANY REASON):

"I really appreciate the offer and I know you just want us to be able to have a good time, but this one makes me uncomfortable and I have to say no. Please don't take it personally."

- **On merging your bank accounts**

"I'm not sure I'm ready for that."

"The mere notion of anyone else being involved in how I manage my money and pay my bills has caused me intense, suffocating distress. Seriously, look at me. I'm hyperventilating. *OMGICAN'T DOITICAN'TDOIT.*"*

---

* This may or may not be what I said to my husband right before we got married. Reader: we did not merge our bank accounts.

OPTIONAL NO-FOR-NOW:
"At this moment, I'm inclined to keep our finances separate, but I'm happy to revisit the idea in [an alternate timeframe]."

- **On being asked to sacrifice or put your career on hold for theirs**

  "I've thought a lot about it, and I don't believe I can do that and still be happy in our relationship. I hope we can work things out another way."

- **On supporting them financially**

It's possible that you originally signed on to be the major (or sole) breadwinner and you may have been happy with that arrangement. But over time, or in tough or unusual circumstances, it may no longer be the right—or feasible—arrangement. You're allowed to rethink major lifestyle matters, and you also can't will your salary to double in size just because someone else lost their job or wants to abandon it to get an MFA in jazz performance.

If it's so they can go back to school for further education:

"I so wish I could afford to cover all of our costs, but I've done the numbers and it's just not possible. I'm happy to help brainstorm other ways to make it work though."

If it's so they can pursue a dream job that doesn't pay very well:

See above.

If it's so they can stay home with your kids:

See above, above.

If it's due to a sudden job loss:

See above, above, above.

If it's after a prolonged period of supporting them already:

"Unfortunately, I'm not going to be able to do this anymore. It's time for us to come up with another solution."

If it's digging them out of a single major hole of their own doing:

"I'm really sorry you're going through this, but I can't be the one to bail you out. It's just beyond my ability/comfort level."

Or if you've just realized your significant other is a moron/pathological liar/criminal...

"WHAT. THE. FUCK. You're on your own and I'll take my keys back and a restraining order out if I have to."

And last but not least...

- **On having sex if you can't, shouldn't, or just don't want to**

I'm fairly sure we went over this on pages 167 to 170, but to reiterate: **"No" should always be enough,** for someone you just met at a Packers tailgate or someone with whom you've been living in wedded bliss for more than half your life.

FOR ANY REASON.

If you want to *give* that reason — such as "I'm really tired" or "I don't feel so great about my body right now" or "Your breath smells like a bison's ball sack" — that's up to you. It might help ease the tension. And it should put an end to the discussion until someone learns how to use toothpicks. Seriously, are we aging beef jerky in there?

(See also: inconsequential fibbing to spare someone's feelings, page 64.)

But maybe the reason you don't want to have sex right now is because the sex you've *been having* with your partner isn't to your liking and you're not sure how to bring that up, so you're stalling. This seems somewhat counter productive for all involved, but okay. Again, "No" should be sufficient until you gather the wherewithal and perhaps some accompanying props or visual aids with which to say **"I would like to try something a little different this time."**

But if your reason is **"We have other relationship problems that need to be addressed before I am going to want to have/feel comfortable having sex with you,"** then, per page 218, you should probably get that out in the open sooner rather than later. It might make for a tense or awkward conversation (or let's be real, multiple conversations), but the fact remains that **two people cannot fix a problem that one of them doesn't know they have.**

Or three people, for that matter. I don't know how your relationship works and I do not judge.

Other relationship problems that may need to be addressed before you want to have sex with someone today, tomorrow, more frequently, or ever again: a sampling

Someone hasn't been super nice lately

Someone doesn't listen to someone else

Someone's acting awfully selfish

Someone sure does party a lot

Someone has commitment issues

✳ ✳ ✳

Depending on your situation, my assessments and advice may seem right on the nose, feel too close for comfort, or be a hot and heavy combination of the two. That's because **sex and relationships — and your relationship to sex — are wicked complicated and unique** and I do not have all of the answers. If I did, I would be writing very different kinds of books, although they would probably still have "fuck" in the titles.

All I can do is a) reassure you that you're not alone in your problems and b) throw down some straight-dope common sense for you to pick up and put into foreplay as you see fit.

Also, c) just gonna keep reminding you that you are entitled to say no to sex FOR ANY REASON.

And if you need help shaping your argument, FuckNotes are here for you. (In a totally platonic way.)

FuckNotes: Partners Edition

Gather the following:

- Term of endearment (e.g., "Babe" or "Snookums")
- Thing you've been asked to do
- Corresponding verb
- An alternate suggestion/solution
- An alternate timeframe in which you could do it (optional)

If you CAN'T

I'm, sorry _____, but I can't _____
            term of endearment   *verb*

_____. Maybe we/you could _____?
thing you've   *alternate suggestion/*
been asked to do   *solution*

[Or if it can wait, I'd be happy to do it

_____.]
time period, i.e. "later"
or "in a few weeks"

If you SHOULDN'T

I'm, sorry _____, but that's not a good
              term of endearment

idea for me. Maybe we/you could _____?
                                   alternate suggestion/solution

[I don't mind if you _____ _____
                          verb   *thing you've been*
                                     asked to do

without me though!]

If you JUST DON'T WANT TO

My   dear   sweet   _____,   I   really
_____term of endearment_____

don't   want   to   do   that.   [I   don't   mind   if   you

_____ _____ without me though!]
verb   thing you've been
                  asked to do

FAMILY

parents, siblings, extended family,
children, in-laws, and everything
they want from you all life long

Each of the preceding chapters has helped you begin to navigate the kinds of issues that may arise with your family—such as declining to join your mom's bridge club or to read your brother's urologist's manuscript. And that's good progress, but I'm assuming your no muscles will require a bit more focused and strenuous workout before you can flex them fully in the faces of your kinfolk.

Just a hunch.

Lucky for you, I happen to be very good at saying no to my family. I am also very good at saying no to my husband's family and to our nieces and nephews—and so far I haven't been disowned, disinherited, divorced, or asked to leave anyone's house after honestly and politely telling their four-year-old "No, I do not want to play *Cars.*"

So in this final fucking chapter, consider me the Mickey Goldmill to your Rocky Balboa. We'll bob and weave through **bold requests**; deadlift **unreasonable demands**; hoist **hosting duties**; put our glutes into **group gifts, guilt trips,** and **going home for the holidays**; and run **intervals on inopportune times for a video chat, Mom.**

Look Ma, [these are my] no hands!

I've said it before and I'll say it again:

> **Ultimately, your family are just people,
> and it's okay to say no to them.***

If you prick them, do they not bleed? If you tickle them, do they not laugh? And if you politely decline to attend your cousin's wedding, did they not literally give you the option to say no right there on the RSVP card?

They so do, and they so did.

It would behoove you to keep this in mind when you're struggling to deny a family member something they've asked for and which you cannot, should not, or do not want to give.

Another helpful thing to keep in mind is: **how would you want *them* to handle this situation if your roles were reversed?**

I don't know about you, but I don't relish the idea of my family saying yes when they don't want to do something or showing up when they don't want to be somewhere, and I'm happy for them to be honest about that. If they don't feel comfortable being honest, they can just be polite and that's fine too. **They shouldn't feel guilty about**

---

* This is, in fact, the subject of an entire chapter in my book *You Do You*: http://nofucksgivenguides.com/ydy/

making those kinds of decisions, and neither do I when I treat them exactly the way I would want to be treated.

It's a solid rule. Golden, you might say.

However, before anybody gets to treating anybody with honesty and politeness, somebody has to make a decision about whether to say no in the first place. Don't be nervous — you've done this before. Per the guidelines and "Do I really *have* to" flowchart on page 59: is this an **I MUST** or an **I SHOULD?** And in the end, **WILL YOU?**

> Do you have to be there for your brother's lacrosse tourney three states over, or is it objectively okay to sit this one out?

> Is your daughter going to be irreparably damaged if you say she cannot have a cherry red scooter, or are you just being a pushover?

> Should you say yes when your parents ask you to drive them to the airport, or, given that their flight is at 6 a.m. on your day off, would arranging a taxi be a reasonable compromise?

Once you settle on your answer, I can help you drop and give me twenty ways to express it. We'll warm up with an offshoot of the PARTNERS chapter, since **someone else's family — however proximate to you — should be easier to say no to than your own.**

Scenari-nos: in-laws

For the purposes of this section, "in-laws" shall refer to any and all family of your partner — whether you're three hookups in or already joined in holy matrimony.

It's never too early to set boundaries.

They're parents, but not *your* parents. Siblings but not *your* siblings. And I know this might sound crazy, but…you don't have to acquiesce to in-law requests just because you happen to have married into their clan — or because you're dating into their clan with or without the potential of future legal association.

The trick with extra-familial naysaying is to reflect on everything I've already taught you, including Why Yes/When No, weighing warranted vs. unwarranted guilt, and boning up on your flowchart game with regard to obligation. Then add one last diagnostic:

Do *I* have to say this no?
(Or can my partner handle it?)

- **Some in-law requests will be directed specifically at you and are yours and only yours to accept or decline.**

Examples include: "Would you like to join us for a girls' day at the spa?" or "Can I put my client in touch with you who's written a memoir about his lifelong passion for seahorses?" or "How come you never want to participate in our Hugging Circle?" To which you might say:

"Thanks so much for including me, but I have to pass."

OPTIONAL NO-AND-SWITCH:
"I have to pass, but maybe we could do X [or better yet, Y] [at a different time] instead?"

"That's not something I'm interested in, but I appreciate you thinking of me."

"Doing things the way your family does them doesn't come naturally to me. I hope you understand where I'm coming from, and that we can continue along in our largely separate but merry ways."

• **But other asks, invitations, and the like will be directed at you as a couple, and perhaps it's in everyone's best interests if your partner fields those.**

"In sickness, health, and emails written in the 'we' form" — isn't that how the vows go? Here are some things you could say to your significant other so *they* can deal with it:

If YOU want to say no:

"I don't want to do this, but I totally understand if you want to participate without me. I'd love it if you could handle the reply for both of us and just tell them I can't make it."

"As it turns out, I'd prefer not to spend four hours brunching with your racist uncle. You can do what you want, but unless you'd like me to say that *specifically,* I'm going to need you to RSVP on our behalf. Thanks, babe!"

If BOTH OF YOU want to say no:

"Great, please let them know."

"If you don't feel like you can tell your parents the truth, just don't blame me for it, okay? I'll be happy to help concoct an alternative that does not result in yours truly spending the next ten years reclining under a metaphorical bus."

How you feelin', Rock? Ready to chase a motherfucking chicken around the yard? Good, because that's often what it feels like to deal with the youngest members of your family. Let's hit it!

Scenari-nos: kiddos

I am not a parent. And if you think that makes me unqualified to give advice about saying no to your little tater tots, I will not be offended if you decide to skip this section.

However, please note that by the same logic you may also wish to stop taking pointers from lots of people who have thoughtfully interacted with but do not themselves possess the thing

Things your child may ask you for that you can't, shouldn't, or don't want to give

Stuff
Money
Permission
More (time, candy, etc.)
That pretty much covers it

they are giving you advice about, such as male gynecologists, Best Buy employees who don't have their own fifty-inch flat-screen Samsungs, and architects who have never actually lived in a Colonial but are happy to charge you an exorbitant fee to tell you exactly how you should go about restoring yours.

Totally your call.

WWSKD

I may not have kids myself, but I do have seven nieces and nephews, two first cousins once removed, and countless friends with countless youngsters among them—and let me tell you, Naughty Aunt Sarah has a strong track record of taking the air out of teen angst, stopping toddlers from commandeering the airplane window shade, and getting third-graders to quit begging for ice cream and eat their goddamn hot dog first.

What's my secret? I gave it some thought when I sat down to write this section, and here's what I came up with:

Maybe you feel guilty about saying no when your child wants a bunny.
But *I* don't.

Maybe you're worried they'll hate you forever for denying them ten more minutes of playing outside before they absolutely must take a bath.
But *I'm* not.

Maybe you're so old and tired and worn down that you no longer possess the will to fight over what constitutes a "reasonable" curfew.

But *I* do.

In conclusion, I probably find it easier to say no to children *because* they do not belong to me. Makes sense. I've got no guilt, no fear, no susceptibility to their puppy-dog eyes, and no patience for their bullshit.

So here's a wacky idea…

Perhaps one way you could begin successfully saying no to your kids is to **pretend you're ME saying no to SOMEONE ELSE'S kids!**

(What? Role-playing games have been known to perk up many a relationship; I see no reason they couldn't revolutionize yours with that be-diapered devil you invited into your home.)

All kidding aside though, just as an exercise: the next time you reach the end of your parental tether — instead of giving in to whatever demand is on the docket — how about you **channel your favorite child-free anti-guru for emotional support** and see what happens. We'll call this game **What Would Sarah Knight Do?***

---

* She would be blunt, firm, and occasionally saucy, and sometimes would bend the truth a teensy bit because it amuses her and isn't hurting anybody.

WWSKD

REQUEST	RESPONSE
"Can we go to the zoo?"	"That's a negative for today, ya little monkey."
"Can I have more candy?"	"No. There's a finite supply of candy in the world so if you eat it all now, we'll have to cancel Halloween."
"Can Jimmy come over?"	"Nope, but feel free to ask me again if Jimmy ever gets less annoying."
"*Ugh*, can you stop being so *LAME?!*"	"Sorry, it's my sworn duty."
"Can I just watch one more episode?"	"No, studies have shown that one more episode will rot your still-forming brain and I can't have that on my conscience."
"Can you stop talking to your friend and pay attention to me, me, and only meeeeeee???"	"It's rude to interrupt people, so I'm going to ask you to please simmer down and let me finish my conversation, m'kay?"

As far as I can tell, you've got nothing to lose by trying — except perhaps another battle with your mini-me over whether it's okay to enter your bedroom uninvited at 6 a.m. to reenact the plot of *Frozen*. If that's your idea of an acceptable wake-up call, have at it. If not, try this: **"Knock. Just knock. Why aren't you knocking? Do you know how to knock?"***

Real talk is the new baby talk

Another of my tactics for fruitful interaction with children is to treat them the same way I would treat someone in the upper age brackets, minus the cursing. Mostly. I realize that toddlers may not appreciate all the nuances of why I don't want to play Drop the Spoon with them. ("No, because every time you drop it, I have to pick it up. We don't get to change sides, which makes this a much less fun game for me than it is for you. I am not going to pick up the spoon again. If you drop it and never get it back and that upsets you, you can't say I didn't warn you.") But my feeling is that the sooner they get exposed to life's little disappointments, the sooner they'll learn to accept them with dignity and aplomb. Also I really fucking hate Drop the Spoon.

No, But

If you thought the No-and-Switch was great for friends and coworkers, have you *met* kids? They're so ripe for the picking they might as well be September grapes in the Côte des Blancs region. Half the time they don't even really want whatever they're asking you for anyway;

---

* This is a line Auntie Sarah paraphrased from *Frozen* itself. Told ya there's a movie quote or song lyric for all your no-ing needs.

they just want *something*. You can easily manipulate — um, I mean, **redirect them into an alternate outcome** that works better for you.

You can even **give them a choice between *multiple* outcomes** that would work better for you. You're granting them agency, which sounds like something actual parenting books would recommend.

How? Well, you may have heard of "Yes, And." It's a game that improv comedians play to sharpen their collaboration skills. No matter how bizarre an idea one actor introduces, their partner has to play along to keep the scene alive and entertaining.

My version is called "No, But." Its express purpose is to end the scene.

NO, BUT

REQUEST	RESPONSE
"Can we go to the zoo?"	"No, but I'll buy you a *National Geographic* subscription and you can read it whenever you want."
"Can I have more candy?"	"No, but you can have more chicken OR broccoli."
"Can Jimmy come over?"	"No, but you can go over to Jimmy's. Have fun!"
"*Ugh*, can you stop being so *LAME?!*"	"No, but I promise to be extra lame when you least expect it. Unless you'd like to take that back?"

| "Can I just watch one more episode?" | "No, but I'll make you a deal: you can watch two tomorrow if you start well before bedtime, or you can watch none at all tomorrow if you keep whining about it tonight. Choose wisely." |
| "Can you stop talking to your friend and pay attention to me, me, and only meeeeeee???" | "No, but you are more than welcome to apologize for interrupting us, after which you may amuse yourself quietly for ten more minutes. Deal?" |

As I'm sure you've noticed, my kiddo scenari-nos revolve mainly around the juvenile of the species. This is by design. If you start 'em young, you won't have so many difficult, guilt-ridden no's to say down the line when your aging offspring already know better than to push their luck. It's the no that keeps on no-ing!

But if *Fuck No!* didn't hit shelves in time to help you train your now-adult spawn in the ways of WWSKD or "No, But," you can still bust out my little reindeer games. Who's going to stop you? The thirty-one-year-old who still lives at home and needs a ride to Jimmy's house to work on their podcast?

Lastly, bear in mind that as with any ill-conceived yes,* **if you give in to your kid in the short-term because you think it's easier —**

---

* Yes, I'm proud of that pun.

whether to stop them begging, whining, or screaming, or just to alle-viate your own guilt — **it may not work out so well for you in the long term.** Children are burgeoning autocrats from Day One. If you give an inch, they will take the Crimean Peninsula.

I'm not saying you should riot in the streets to depose them, but learning how to deliver a firm, effective no is a step in the right direction.

Scenari-nos: parents and siblings, round one

Now that we've built up your strength and stamina on your "chosen family" (partners and children and in-laws by default), we're gonna take it to the mat with those you in no way *chose* to be related to — and yet they're among the hardest to say no to, because guilt and obligation are fun like that.

I understand that it can be tough to neg someone who changed your diapers or dutifully picked you up from soccer practice every afternoon for three years in the late eighties. That's some Deep State guilt and obligation right there. And parents occupy a unique position in our cultural hierarchy as **Those Who Must Be Obeyed.** When you're fifteen and living under mom's roof, "Can you please turn down the music?" is not so much a request as a directive — and saying no is not only rude, it'll probably result in **consequences that aren't worth your act of rebellion.**

Whereas if you're forty-five and taking time off work to come home for a visit and your dad asks if you want to spend it re-bricking his shed, I feel **you've earned some decision-making autonomy** (see page 248).

It's similar with siblings. You may have grown up doing everything together and to this day you share a special, unbreakable bond — or maybe all you share is a set of matching scars from your simultaneous bouts of chicken pox back in '75.

But either way, having hatched from the same womb or been raised by one or more of the same parents **doesn't obligate you to say yes to your sister for life.** Especially when she's being fucking ridiculous.

So for the fifteenth (and final) time: if it's your heart's desire to do things with and for your parents, take your sister up on her unsolicited advice, or let your little bro crash at your place indefinitely — that's cool. **I'm not here to drive a stake through functional family dynamics.**

However, **if you CAN'T, SHOULDN'T, or DON'T WANT TO — it's okay to say no.** You can even blame me if you have to. I get paid for this.

Let's go nuclear, shall we?

• **Hosting duties**

With regard to holidays and other family affairs, do you feel like your parents and/or siblings aren't pulling their weight in the "plan, prep, have everyone over, and clean up after them while they chat amongst themselves and Dad farts up my living room" department? Do you do it every single time? Or did you do it once and that was QUITE

ENOUGH, THANK YOU? In any case, avoid getting involuntarily location-scouted again with one of these trusty comebacks:

If you can't:

"I wish I could, but I just don't have the time to handle everything this year."

"My place isn't really big enough for everybody to enjoy themselves and be comfortable."

"My cats simply will not allow it."

If you shouldn't:

"I'd love to have everyone over, but I have to work the next morning and if I'm hosting it's just too long a day for me."

"My landlord is very strict about large groups. She's not just down there banging on her ceiling with a broomstick for her health."

If you just don't want to:

"I just don't want to."

OPTIONAL NO-AND-SWITCH:
"I'd be happy to help [plan/shop/cook/etc.] but I'd rather not have it at my place. Let me know what you decide!"

- **Group gifts**

Are you just a teensy bit tired of your sibling(s) proposing a "joint" Mother's Day gift, knowing that means they expect you to come up with the idea, do the shopping, and pay for it?

> "I'm gonna go my own way this year."

> "I already gave her my gift."

If you feel you can be blunt:

> "No, I don't want to do that because I'll end up dealing with it and you'll just sit back and take credit. Sorry, but you know it's true. Love ya!"

---

3 responses to "Are you sure you don't want seconds?"

"No thank you, I'm full."

"The meal was delicious, and my goal is to think back on it fondly, without a stomachache."

"Perhaps I didn't speak clearly because I was still chewing the last massive 'bite' you put on my plate, but I'm really not hungry anymore, I swear to the sanctified corpse of that chicken you so artfully roasted in my honor."

- **If I were you, I'd be sure Joey spends at least twenty minutes a day listening to birdsong to help develop his cognitive skills.**

It makes sense that the experienced parents who already parented you would have tips for parenting your kids, too. Same with brothers and sisters who got to this stage ahead of you. And sometimes such tips are welcome. (Here's a tip: free babysitting is *always* welcome.) But if the suggestions are coming a little too fast and furious, it's okay to pump the brakes.

"I know you mean well, but telling me everything I should be doing — and implying that what I *am* doing isn't enough — isn't exactly helping."

"I really value your insight, but for what it's worth, I'm also kind of looking forward to figuring this stuff out on my own."

"Thanks, I'll keep that in mind!"

- **But they're your nieces and nephews!**

If, like me, you do not enjoy being surrounded by shrieking children with their sticky hands and their endless fidgeting, you may also not enjoy showing up to family gatherings where such behavior thrives and is indeed often encouraged. Your family may know this about you, yet somehow think your aversion is suspended when it comes to the flesh of their flesh. It isn't.

When your parents *insist:*

"I love you, but this is not fun for me. Enjoy your grandchildren and I'll see you another time."

When your siblings *insist:*

"I love you, but you know how I feel about kids. It's better for all of us if I pass."

Ding ✱ Ding ✱ Ding

You know what that sound means — we've hit the end of round one. You're doing great! Let's do a little bag work to keep you in the zone...

Branching out: extended family scenari-nos

Perhaps your family tree includes aunts, uncles, cousins, and their ilk who pop up in your inbox or on your doorstep from time to time asking for things you can't, shouldn't, or don't want to give them. Well, guess what? I have already supplied you with words to use for passing on Uncle Jamal's pig roast or declining Cousin Tammy's suggestion that you host an essential oils party at your apartment. They're the same words with which you say no to anyone's pig roasts and patchouli parties:

"No."

"No thank you."

"Alas, I'm not available that day!"

But lest I be seen as shirking my guru-ly duties, here are a few more phrases to draw upon when delivering an extended family negatory:

"Sorry to miss this — say hi to [other family member/s] for me!"

"Unfortunately, third cousins are ineligible for the family discount. I know, so weird, right?"

"I'm sure your kids *would* look awfully cute in their miniature formalwear, but our wedding is adults-only. Yes, even for family."

"I haven't seen you in fifteen years and your nephew is no longer married to my sister, so no, I will not cosign your mortgage."

Is the beach house free this weekend?

I realize this is a rare and privileged position to be in, but I like to be thorough, so here goes: if you happen to have worked hard enough and/or been lucky-as-fuck enough to come into possession of an extremely valuable item, YOU ARE UNDER NO OBLIGATION TO LET YOUR FAMILY MEMBERS USE IT — FOR FREE OR AT ALL. You *can*, but you do not *have to*. Cousins are just as likely to trash your vacation home or bash up your boat or dent the doors of your sweet, sweet luxury SUV as anyone. They are only human, and humans make mistakes, and some humans are just irresponsible assholes. Maybe you're related to a few. If so, they can pay rent and take out insurance and put down security deposits just like the rest of the world, or they can take no for an answer while your Jet Ski remains intact and in your garage.

Ding ✳ *Ding* ✳ *Ding*

Here we go again. Get those gloves up!

Scenari-nos: parents and siblings, round two

- **Togetherness. SO MUCH TOGETHERNESS.**

Your family might take vacations together, renting one big cabin for everybody to go to sleep in together at night and wake up in together every morning. Or maybe you just all pile into your parents' house together for the holidays and do it up old school. Togetherness can be great fun. Yay, togetherness!

But perhaps **your tolerance for the *level* of togetherness** differs from that of your parents or siblings. And perhaps you are forty years old and can absolutely afford an Airbnb, or you have children of your own that you'd prefer to sequester in a hotel room to ensure they go to bed and stay asleep instead of playing group grab-ass with their cousins 'til the wee hours. And maybe you expressed as much to your parents and/or siblings and they scoffed or blanched or gasped, and then tried to pressure you into doing it their way — because their way works just fine for them even if it leaves you stressed, sleepless, and unable to take your "morning constitutional" in peace.*

If they're paying for it and you can't afford to go your own way:

"I can't tell you how much I appreciate you hosting the annual pilgrimage to Antelope Alley, but I have to be really honest and clear with you that I'm not at a point in my life where I can

---

* Pooping. I'm talking about pooping.

handle a six-day slumber party with our entire family. I'm going to pass this year, not because I don't love you or appreciate your generosity, but because I need to focus on my own well-being for now. I hope you understand."

If you could *pay to go your own way but they don't* want *you to:*

"I'd like to try something new for this [vacation/holiday]. Having my/our own space to decompress helps me be more refreshed and present for the rest of the time we all spend together, and for me that's worth the expense."

- **Visiting at inopportune times and/or places**

Depending on how far away you live from your family, you may be discouraging drop-ins at your apartment or trying to plan *rendezvous* that don't render you panicking at the prospect of Mom and Dad having an unsupervised conversation with your roommate in the dorms. Maybe your brother likes to show up at your office to "hang out while you work" and your sister has a gift for swinging by while you're up to your neck in breastfeeding your new baby. Whatever the case, staking out your territory loud and clear works for the mongoose and it can work for you:

"That's not great for me, but I'll see you another time soon."

"We have to talk about 'popping in,' by which I mean please don't."

"I'd prefer to see you [somewhere/sometime] that I'm not distracted by [school/work/a tiny human chomping on my raw and swollen tatas]."

RELATED: When they want to Skype or FaceTime and you are not in the mood for video chatting. (Or perhaps chatting at all.)

"Now isn't a good time for me." (Remember this one from the financial favors section? So succinct! So all-purpose!)

"I haven't [shaved/put on makeup/recovered from my hangover]. You don't want to see this and I don't want to show it to you."

"Guys, I'm naked."

- **Can I get a little help around here?**

Resetting routers and locating all those photos your mom swears must be somewhere in the cloud is a rite of homecoming. Light chores also come with the territory — the same ones you were expected to do when you lived there, and maybe some extras brought on by your dad's advanced age and reduced ability to get up on a ladder and change a light bulb. Or maybe your folks or siblings are in a tight spot financially and a crucial home repair won't get done unless you're able and willing to pitch in and/or pay for it.

However, merely being an able-bodied holiday visitor from out of town — or one who lives in the same town year-round — doesn't mean you have to say yes to hard labor whenever it's convenient for your family to enlist you. They can certainly ask for heavy-duty help, and you can certainly give it if you're so inclined, but if you can't (spend your whole weekend painting), shouldn't (risk your trick knee on a major construction project), or just don't want to (re-grout the bathtub on Christmas Eve), you're allowed to respond in kind.

> "I can see you need help with this. Let's start by me *helping* you call an electrician."

> "I love you, but re-bricking the shed is not my idea of spending quality time together."

> "I'm not really in the mood to lay sod after spending seven hours in Memorial Day weekend traffic, but I bet I can find you a neighbor kid who'll do it if you give him fifty bucks and fair warning."

• Swedish Death Cleaning

Have you heard of this? It's a practice whose charming name refers to shoveling all of one's crap out of one's home when one realizes that one's days are numbered — the goal being to reduce the volume of stuff that one's grieving family has to sort through after the fact. It's a noble effort, but as with garden-variety decluttering, this activity can bring on the fever of giving away "free stuff" to people like *you*. And saying no can feel fraught because you're over here rejecting family heirlooms and relegating childhood mementos to the trash heap and your folks are over there grappling with their own mortality. I understand wanting to make this easier on them, but you are under no obligation to receive or display ugly quilts and old swimming trophies if you don't want to.

"No thanks, you can toss it!"

"I really don't have room for that."

"Oh, that brings back memories. I'm glad you showed it to me, but you can go ahead and put it in the donation bin. I don't mind."

OPTIONAL NO-AND-SWITCH:
"I don't want any of those things, but I'll keep you company while you're cleaning out if you like."

- **You should come home more often.**

Some of us get weepily nostalgic for the smell of our hometown gas station, while others would relegate an entire hemisphere to the rearview mirror if we could. Putting aside for the moment the question of whether you *can* visit "home" more often, in terms of having the means to do so — and assuming your parents understand if you don't — what can you say if you *just don't want to*, but you also don't want to hurt their feelings?

"I miss you too, but I'm building a life here and I need to focus on that for a while. Please don't make me feel guilty about it."

"There's so much of the world I want to see. I hope you understand that for now, going back to [where you came from] isn't my top priority."

"I love you guys, but there's a reason I left, and I'm not ready to go back yet."

Peace offerings

You don't have to slaughter a lamb and arrange it on a pyre on their porch, but you can make gestures toward your family to smooth over any feathers that might get ruffled by your decision to say no. Small ones, like mailing regular post cards when you know you're not going to make it home for a while. Medium ones, like contributing a nice fruit basket to the Cabin of Togetherness when you're staying off-site. Or big, bold declarations of "See, I do love you!" like accepting their friendship on Facebook.

Ding ✻ Ding ✻ Ding

Almost there, champ. Things might get a little more heated in the next round, **and I don't want you to get knocked out by guilt.** One last thing to consider as you square up for the final no-down is that no matter how rationally and politely you say no, **your family members will sometimes *hear it* differently than you intended.**

Like when I'm visiting my brother and his wife in Los Angeles and after an epic five-hour meal I say "I want to go back to my hotel now" and he says "Great, we'll join you at the bar for a nightcap."

Or perhaps more concerning — *

You say: "I don't want to go to church with you anymore because I'm an adult now with my own opinions and I don't really believe in organized religion."

Your parents hear: "You raised a heretic. God will judge you harshly for it and I don't care!" or "I know you spent your life savings on parochial school, but I can't be bothered to even *pretend* to swallow the body and blood a few times a year."

Ultimately, you cannot control how people choose to interpret your no, nor how they react to it. All you can control is *your* decision-making process, *your* delivery, and *your* reaction to their reaction. If you need a quick refresher on guilt, obligation, honesty and politeness, and standing your ground before heading back into the ring for round three, please refer to the guidelines set forth on pages 48, 54, 63, and 104, respectively.

And remember: we don't negotiate with terrorists. You've got this.

Ding ✱ Ding ✱ Ding

---

* Though if you've met my brother, you know you should be VERY concerned about letting him talk you into "one more drink."

Scenari-nos: parents and siblings, round three

- **Time-sharing**

When parents split up or sibling rivalries turn into full-on wars, you may be left trying to please all of the people an exactly equal amount of the time, which is as absurd and impossible as it sounds.

If your estranged family members live near one another and expect you to parcel out every minute of your weekend shuttling among them such that none of *them* get short shrift and *you* don't get a motherfucking moment's peace, then hurling "It's not my fault YOU got divorced!" is one way to handle it, but I think we all know it's not a good look. How about something more like this instead:

> "Just because it's equal time doesn't make it quality time. Let's enjoy ourselves while we're together."

> "Sorry, but you know math was never my best subject!"

> "I love you both. I shouldn't have to prove it by keeping a time sheet."

Whereas if the feud crosses state (or country) lines and you couldn't even hopscotch it if you wanted to — you're gonna have to bust out some no's in different area codes:

On holidays:

"I can't spend [Holiday X] with both of you, so I have to make some difficult choices. This year it's going to be with [other family member/s], okay? I love you."

OPTIONAL NO-AND-SWITCH:
"I'm going to do [Holiday X] with [other family members] this year. I don't have enough [time off/money] to do a separate trip to see you, but if you want to find a time to come here, that would be great."

In general:

"I love you both, but unfortunately there's a limit to the amount of [time/energy/money] I can spend planning and executing double the number of trips and hosting visitors to accommodate the fact that [my parents are divorced/my siblings don't get along/etc.]. I have to draw the line somewhere, and I'm feeling it right now."

● **Can't we all just get along?**

Spats and rough patches are one thing, but some family feuds run too intense to kiss and make up from—or even to be in the same room together during. Your father may wish that you could let your emotionally abusive mother off the hook like he does, or that you'd ignore your brother's sexist comments instead of reading him the Pussy Riot act over dinner. But asking you to overlook or accept bad behavior is just that—an ask. You can say no in a number of ways (including removing yourself from such situations altogether):

"I handle my relationship with [family member] differently than you do, and that's okay."

"I know why you want me to let this go, but I'm not going to do that."

"I can't be around [family member] right now without things boiling over, so I'm going to take a time-out for everyone's sake."

- **Customs or traditions that you don't enjoy/believe in/agree with**

Those Who Must Me Obeyed may have raised you in a faith or doctrine or with certain cultural trappings that, as an adult, you've decided are not really your "thing" — so much so you find it at best unpleasant to participate and, at worst, aggressively repellent or soul-crushing. I'm talking anything from religious practices like praying before a meal or keeping kosher to secular family activities that have become increasingly off-putting in your dotage. Caroling in matching sweaters absolutely qualifies. Fortunately, it's possible to remain respectful to the people you love without getting roped into something that's no longer (if it ever was) in your wheelhouse. For example:

"I think this is the year I say goodbye to [custom/tradition/ritual/practice], but you guys enjoy yourselves and we'll connect [before/after/in a different way]."

"I understand why you want me to be part of this, but it's not really my thing anymore. I think the right way to move forward is to let you do what's best for you and me do what's best for me. Does that seem fair?"

"I don't want to participate in [custom/tradition/ritual/practice] but I respect your desire to do so."

No-Tip: No, but make it a pictogram! Use emojis to keep your no's brief, nonconfrontational, and disarming. "I'd rather choke on a hard-boiled egg than sit through Easter services" becomes "Can't make it this year! [bunny] [ham] [sad face]"

● **Can you tone it down?**

In the same way that you're capable of being respectful of your family's way of life without necessarily joining in, there's no reason they can't be accepting of your facial piercings, your fashion choices, or your general avant-garde aesthetic. (Jeez, why'd they even save your baby teeth if they didn't want you to make a necklace out of them?) In times like these, the all-around leader in Hard No's is as follows:

"Sorry guys, I do me."

But let's say your family's request for you to repress yourself goes further than asking you not to wear your Steve Buscemi onesie to your dad's retirement party.*

---

* https://www.lostateminor.com/2016/04/27/289173/

For example, maybe your parents claim they accept your sexual orientation but ask you not to talk about it in front of their friends, or say that they like your significant other who is of a different race or religious background but ask you not to bring them to cousin Kim's wedding.

As a cis, white, heterosexual woman with liberal parents who don't disapprove openly of or nag me about my life choices, I admit I haven't got much hands-on experience navigating family relationships of this nature. But I don't need to have been directly affected by bigotry and prejudice to say this:

> **You are in no way *obligated* to change or hide your lifestyle to suit the myopic views or beliefs of your family members. THEY are the ones making unreasonable demands here, and YOU are entitled to reject them.**

Instead, try something like this:

> "If I say yes, it's going to hurt me a lot more than it hurts you for me to say no. So, no."

> "I'm surprised and disappointed that you would ask me to do that, and I'm afraid I can't oblige."

> "I want to believe that you don't understand the impact your request has on me, and I hope you'll reconsider, and take it back."

And if your family has *such* severe or radical views about your lifestyle that you feel unsafe expressing yourself or standing up and saying no to them, I hope that someday you'll find your way to another book — or a therapist, counselor, or "chosen family" member — that can help extricate you from those relationships in a safe and healthy manner.

I'm rooting for you, and I bet Steve Buscemi is too.

The "I'll be dead someday" card

Ah, mortality as a misplaced motivator. I'd always thought clutching your hands to your chest, sighing dramatically, and alluding to your eventual death to get your children to do your bidding was just for soap opera screenplays until I saw someone do it with my own two eyes. Damn, that is some flagrant-ass guilt-tripping right there. Put an end to it with some fitting last words of your own:

> "I love you, but my answer is no. And for future reference, that's not the way to convince me to do something for you."

FuckNotes: Family Edition

Here we go again, and for the last time! Prepare to tailor your various, sundry, and eminently justifiable no's into a one-size-fits-all explanation for some of the most special — and especially demanding — people in your life. You will need:

- A salutation (e.g., "Dear" or "Hey") and your family member's name or appellation (e.g., "Walter" or "Dad")

- Their request/demand/offer

- Phrase for fulfilling their request/demand/offer (e.g., "take you up on this" or "be there for you")

- A reason you can't do it (optional)

- An adjective that is the *opposite* of how you're worried they'll feel when you say no

- An alternative to their request (optional)

- An expression of disappointment (e.g., "Bummer," "This sucks," or "Oh shit!")

- A positive verb describing your feelings for this family member

If you CAN'T

_____, _____!
appropriate salutation for this family member, and their name

I wish I could _____, but sadly I
                phrase for fulfilling their request/demand/offer

can't [because _____]. Please don't be
                reason why you can't

_____. I love you!
adjective opposite of how
you worry they will feel

[P.S. Maybe we could _____ instead
                      alternative to their request

sometime soon?]

If you SHOULDN'T

_____, but I'm going to have to say
expression of disappointment

no to _____. I hope you understand—
       their request/demand/offer

it doesn't mean I don't _____ you!
                         verb describing your feelings for them

If you JUST DON'T WANT TO

I have to pass on _____. Love you,
their request/demand/offer

though! Talk soon. XOXO

Epilogue

Well, there you have it, nope fiends. By my calculations, I've provided you with more ways to say no per square inch than the Bible has begats. If *Fuck No!* were a rapper, it would be Lil Wayne. Compact yet prolific.

Are there scenari-nos I haven't managed to address? No doubt. I tried to be creative and inclusive, but if there's anything I've learned from being an author, it's that there's no accounting for the ways in which you can thoroughly disappoint people and inspire them to demand their money back. So I hope that if you didn't see whatever *specific* issue you may have been looking for reflected in these hallowed pages, you've at least picked up plenty of techniques, strategies, and general No-Tips with which to approach it.

Remember: **"Alas!"** is widely applicable; the **No-and-Switch** is a lovely go-to for your next no-go; **Fuck Notes** are your secret weapon; and don't forget your **compliment condiments** — a spoonful of "I can't believe I'm missing out on your legendary salmon loaf" never fails to help the negative go down.

Yes, when it comes to giving no for an answer, I think I've got you covered.

But — and this is just a hypothetical — how about when it comes to *taking* no for an answer YOUR OWN DAMN SELF?

You can't always get what you want: a parable

Once upon a time, your narrator was traveling via subway at that hour of the morning when it seems like every single human in New York City is packed into a steamy steel burrito that's lurching underground at a maddeningly inconsistent pace and temperature in order to deposit the majority of us into the places we loathe most in the world. The only good part about beginning my daily commute fifteen stops deep into Brooklyn was that I was sometimes able to snag a seat halfway through my journey when one sizable round of lemmings decamped in Lower Manhattan. This was one of those blessed days.

At least, it was until a wail rose up from the crowd.

Was it an octogenarian in cardiac arrest? No. Had someone seen a rat? No. Distraught Mets fan? The likeliest of all those scenarios, but also no. The culprit was a five- or six-year-old boy with hair the color of a rusty shed and a passionate desire to sit down.

His campaign had kicked off approximately five minutes earlier with a repetitive but low-decibel request ("Dad, I want to sit.") that morphed into a strident, continuous, human carbon monoxide detector of "DadIwanttositDadIwanttositDadIwantosit."

"No," said Dad, who stood in the doorway across from me, clasping Junior's paw with one hand and a *Wall Street Journal* with the other. "We're getting off soon anyway."

We made another stop or two during which even more humans entered the train and squished together in shared misery. That's when the kid retripled his efforts with an ear-popping ferocity. (No small feat considering most of us had already recalibrated our Eustachian tubes while lingering in a tunnel hundreds of feet beneath the East River.)

"DAD! I! WANT! TO! SIT! DOWN!"

A woman (not me) offered her precious plastic perch — maybe to be nice, but more likely in hopes of ending the onslaught. Dad gallantly refused.

"We only have a couple more stops. Thanks, but it's fine. He'll be fine."

Son of Chucky remained unconvinced that anything would ever be fine again, and let loose a final howl that threatened to strip the ads for Doctor Zizmor's dermatology clinic off the subway like a glycolic peel.

"*DAAAAAD I WANT TO SIT DOOOOWN!!!!!!!*"

Although people were packed between us like asparagus at Trader Joe's, I happened to be eye level with that tiny tyrant. And for one moment, the crush of bodies parted just enough that I could stare directly into his face and say, "Well guess what, buddy? I want you to stop screaming, and we don't always get what we want."

He returned my gaze, slack-jawed as a fresh-caught grouper, and issued nary an additional peep for the remainder of our ride.

The End.

You may be wondering why I chose this particular yarn with which to spin the ending of my Ode to No, when, technically, I did not actually *say* no to the twerpy perp. Nor am I especially proud of the way I handled this situation, which if I'm being honest was a little more Mommie Dearest than Auntie Sarah and thus landed on the wrong end of my preferred politeness spectrum. And it's not to establish further proof of my ability to get other people's children to fall in line, although you have to admit, I'm good at this.

No, I'm closing out *Fuck No!* with this story because in the end, the little rascal *listened*. Not only did he stop running his neck hose, but praise be to subway rats, Dr. Zizmor, and the '86 Mets — he abandoned his quest entirely.

We could all learn a thing or two from that slack-jawed grouper.

Ask? By all means.

Negotiate hard? For sure!

But in the end, ye shall not necessarily receive. Sometimes you'll just have to shut up and suck it up. Sometimes, you have to take no for an answer.

Luckily, every theory, every technique, and every salty anecdote I've presented in this sexy little handbook for *hapana** has prepared you for just that outcome.

---

* That's Swahili for "no."

Yup. This whole time, *Fuck No!* wasn't just for budding naysayers; it was for nay*hearers* too.

You can't afford to take that job for the money they offered you? Totally understandable. Just be ready to accept the same explanation from your coworker who can't let you have those playoff tickets for below face value. Such is life!

You shouldn't be eating the corned beef hash your wife slaved over because it's the night before your annual physical? No problem. I'm sure you won't be a dick about it when your daughter shouldn't be Skyping with you guys after dinner because she needs to go condom-shopping before her date tonight. We've all got priorities!

You don't want to join your politically active friends at a rally? Abso-fucking-lutely fine. Please also respect the wishes of the next person who begs off of participating in *your* pet cause. Not everybody can, should, or wants to save the endangered short-nosed sea snakes. To each their own!

See what I did there?

Your life will improve immeasurably if you can learn to accept no with the same lucidity and composure with which I've spent the last 265 pages teaching you how to proffer it. And so will the lives of people you care about, live and work with, and who just want to ride the F train each morning without incident.

You could start small, by adding a "No pressure!" to the next invitation you extend. Some form of "I'd love to see you but understand if you can't make it" pre-relieves any guilt your guests might be experiencing if they have to say no. It's also a good mantra for you to adopt as a host: a way of looking at all of your parties and events and dinners and celebrations as fun and enjoyable and successful and lovely even if not every single person you invited can attend—and especially if everyone who *does* attend is there UNDER NO UNDUE PRESSURE TO DO SO.

Won't that be pleasant?

Also, perhaps you could think twice before you ask that next favor. I'm not saying you should never ask for help; only suggesting you ruminate briefly on whether what you're about to ask, and of whom, is reasonable. Are you seeking ten thousand dollars in seed money from your wealthy aunt to get your Swedish food truck up and running? And do you have a solid business plan to share with her?

Or are you just looking for an intro to a friend of a friend to soft-pitch them as a potential investor in the MeatballMobile?

Perform a little "do unto others" visualization. Would you find it super annoying or deeply uncool to be asked the same favor? (There is no right answer here—you could be a rich relation who wouldn't lend $10K to even their favorite nephew, or you could be a Gladwellian connector who gives out contact info like extra lingonberry jam on the side, no charge.)

Just, you know, think about it.

If you decide to proceed, note that prefacing your favor request with "I totally understand if you can't help me with this" is actually an effective method of *getting* someone to help you with this. In his book, *Influence: The Psychology of Persuasion,* Dr. Robert B. Cialdini notes that "reciprocity" and "liking" are two principles that will serve you well in this regard—basically, if you're nice about asking, people are more likely to be nice about granting.

Or at least more likely to be less or not-at-all annoyed with you *for* asking, which is good for maintaining jovial relationships with friends, family, colleagues, and near-total strangers.

When seeking consent, respect people's boundaries. It's just not that hard.

In professional situations, play to win, but be ready to graciously accept defeat. You may not get the raise, the promotion, the performance, or the price you were hoping for, but it's a long game out there. Being gallant, respectful, and cool in the face of *No* could very well gain you a second chance at *Yes.* And it keeps the rest of us from having to gossip about and blacklist that boss, colleague, client, customer, or vendor who hurl their toys out of the pram every time they don't get what they want. Be an adult, and move on.

In romantic relationships, recognize that your "other half" is an individual in their own right. You can go your own way sometimes, and let them go theirs.

And finally, savor your interactions with your family. Don't begrudge them the hours or days or spring breaks they can't, shouldn't, or don't want to spend together. All that does is poison the time you *do* have and make them want to *spend even less of it with you* being harassed, harangued, or quietly resented for their life decisions over what might otherwise have been a nice meal or game of Scrabble.

My goal has always been for you to develop a new appreciation for no *from all sides*. I hope *Fuck No!* has given you the confidence and language with which to convey it, but also the attitude and perspective to be able to hear it and take it to heart. The more we issue and receive thoughtful, necessary no's, the more all of us will be living honestly, politely, and respectfully — for ourselves and others.

We'll experience more relief and less guilt, leading to more pleasurable and less onerous interactions.

We'll be grateful for success and prepared for disappointment.

We'll value ourselves and others as we and others deserve to be valued: each as individuals with unique difficulties, needs, and desires that do not — and cannot possibly be expected to — line up perfectly with everyone else's at all times.

This is the joy of no. Learn it. Live it. And for fuck's sake: **SAY IT.**

You'll be glad you did.

STOP
SAYING
YES

WHEN YOU
WANT TO
SAY
FUCK NO!

Acknowledgments

For five No Fucks Given Guides now, I've had the privilege to work with the same core group of phenomenal talent in my literary agent and my U.S. and U.K. editors. The four of us are basically the U2 of publishing — improbably and remarkably still going strong in an industry rife with turnover.

(And yes, I have ideas about which specific member of U2 each of us would be, and no, I am not going to commit them to print. You just never know if someone would have strong feelings about being Larry Mullen Jr.)

Long before the NFGGs were a glimmer in my mind and many years before Jennifer Joel was appointed cohead of the entire publishing division at ICM Partners (Brava, JJ!), my future agent told me to come to her with anything I might want to write. She was sure I had a book in me, she said. The first idea I dropped on her was a fuck-filled parody of a Japanese tidying guide, and she didn't even flinch, because she is a stone-cold boss (see: newly minted cohead of ICM Partners) and also very good at predicting bestsellers. I owe her my career and I am grateful every day for her guidance, her friendship, and her excellent taste in celebratory wine.

Back when he was a fresh new editorial recruit at Little, Brown and Company, Michael Szczerban acquired *The Life-Changing Magic of Not Giving a Fuck* — and today he is the motherfucking publisher of his own motherfucking IMPRINT. My work has thrived once again in his capable hands, but this time we added *his* baby, Voracious Books, to the cover. Congratulations, Mike, and I thank you for your ongoing appetite for fuckery, punnery, and portmant*neaus*.

The first communication I ever received from my U.K. editor, Jane Sturrock, contained the words "I mean, come on, seriously. Fuck yoga." I knew from that moment that we'd make a great team, but I couldn't have foreseen that, years later, we'd be at the top of Carmelite House in London, raising our glasses to a million copies sold and going strong. And in addition to her visionary savvy, I'll have you know that Jane is responsible for all of the parts in my books where you could have thought, *Wow, that was a little bitchy, even for Sarah Knight*, but instead you just nodded and laughed, because she had already politely suggested I tone it down a notch before it went to print. A true stealth operator. Thank you, Jane.

I'm also endlessly indebted to Jenn's, Mike's, and Jane's respective colleagues (none of whom, I'm sure, would ever deign to take advantage of one another's good nature to finish a project because they were too hungover to do it themselves). They are:

Loni Drucker, Josie Freedman, Cara Hayes, Tia Ikemoto, Lindsay Samakow, and Sarah Wax at ICM Partners.

Ben Allen, Reagan Arthur, Martha Bucci, Sabrina Callahan,

Raylan Davis, Nicky Guerreiro, Lauren Harms, Brandon Kelley, Laura Mamelok, Suzanne Marx, Katharine Meyers, Meg Miguelino, Amanda Orozco, Deri Reed, Imani Seymour, Kim Sheu, and Craig Young at Little, Brown and Company and Voracious Books; Lisa Cahn, my producer at Hachette Audio; Patrick Smith, my director; and Patrick Geeting, my audio editor at Audiomedia Production.

Katya Ellis, Charlotte Fry, Elizabeth Masters, Laura McKerrell, Ana McLaughlin, Dave Murphy, and Hannah Winter at Quercus Books.

And the folks at Hachette Canada, Australia, and New Zealand who've been with me since the beginning and helped put the NFGGs on bestseller lists in every single goddamn hemisphere.

Thank you all, from the bottom of my Aperol spritz!

Beyond the professional assistance from my publishing team, I get daily sustenance from readers like you and Halle Berry who post pics and send DMs and emails and Instagram Stories telling me how much you love the No Fucks Given Guides or that your dog ate one of them. I truly appreciate it. I even appreciate the occasional hate mail because it keeps me on my toes and gives me something to tweet vengefully about, which is one of my favorite pastimes.

I'd also like to thank my parents, Tom and Sandi Knight, both retired elementary school teachers from whom I must have somehow inherited my ability to get children to fall in line, even if I developed my own spin along the way. (I promise, it's my own spin. Mr. and Mrs. Knight did not make long and distinguished careers out of the...unorthodox practices I detail in this book.)

Finally, thank you to Judd Harris: husband, webmaster, personal chef, and reluctant cat *padrastro*. His behind-the-scenes contributions to the NFGGs are legion. He named the NotSorry Method, he gave us all personal policies, and whenever I need another example of "a thing you might say no to that isn't related to work or family and can't be food-based because I just made a joke in this paragraph about Doritos," he can be counted on to text me a list of options within ten minutes. And also to bring me a bowl of Doritos.

Fuck yes, babe! We did it again.

Index

Page numbers of illustrations appear in italics

About the Author

Sarah Knight's first book, *The Life-Changing Magic of Not Giving a Fuck*, has been published in more than thirty languages, and her TEDx talk, "The Magic of Not Giving a F*ck" has more than six million views. All of the books in her No Fucks Given Guides series have been international bestsellers, including *Get Your Shit Together*, which was on the *New York Times* bestseller list for sixteen weeks. Her writing has also appeared in *Glamour, Harper's Bazaar, Marie Claire, Red, Refinery29*, and elsewhere. After quitting her corporate job to pursue a freelance life, she moved from Brooklyn, New York, to the Dominican Republic, where she currently resides with her husband, two feral rescue cats, and a shitload of lizards.

You can learn more and sign up for her newsletter at nofucksgivenguides.com, follow Sarah on Twitter and Instagram @MCSnugz, and follow the books @NoFucksGivenGuides (Facebook and Instagram) and @NoFucksGiven (Twitter).

Also available

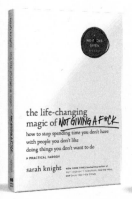

Praise for Sarah Knight

"Genius" —*Cosmopolitan*

"Self-help to swear by." —*Boston Globe*

"Hilarious and truly practical." —*Booklist*